SILVER EDITION

Interactions 2

PARAGRAPH DEVELOPMENT AND INTRODUCTION TO THE ESSAY

WRITING

Cheryl Pavlik
Margaret Keenan Segal

Lawrence J. Zwier
Contributor, Focus on Testing

Meredith Pike-Baky
Writing Strand Leader

Interactions 2 Writing, Silver Edition

Published by McGraw-Hill ESL/ELT, a business unit of The McGraw-Hill Companies, Inc., 1221 Avenue of the Americas, New York, NY 10020.

ISBN 13: 978-0-07-353386-5 (Student Book)
ISBN 10: 0-07-353386-6
1 2 3 4 5 6 7 8 9 10 VNH 11 10 09 08 07 06

Editorial director: Erik Gundersen
Series editor: Valerie Kelemen
Developmental editor: Jennifer Wilson Cooper
Production manager: Juanita Thompson
Production coordinators: Vanessa Nuttry, James D. Gwyn
Cover designer: Robin Locke Monda
Interior designer: Nesbitt Graphics, Inc.
Photo researcher: Photoquick Research

The credits section for this book begins on page iv and is considered an extension of the copyright page.

Cover photo: Bob Krist/Corbis

A Special Thank You

The Interactions/Mosaic Silver Edition team wishes to thank our extended team: teachers, students, administrators, and teacher trainers, all of whom contributed invaluably to the making of this edition.

Macarena Aguilar, **North Harris College**, Houston, Texas ■ Mohamad Al-Alam, **Imam Mohammad University**, Riyadh, Saudi Arabia ■ Faisal M. Al Mohanna Abaalkhail, **King Saud University**, Riyadh, Saudi Arabia; Amal Al-Toaimy, **Women's College, Prince Sultan University**, Riyadh, Saudi Arabia ■ Douglas Arroliga, **Ave Maria University**, Managua, Nicaragua ■ Fairlie Atkinson, **Sungkyunkwan University**, Seoul, Korea ■ Jose R. Bahamonde, **Miami-Dade Community College**, Miami, Florida ■ John Ball, **Universidad de las Americas**, Mexico City, Mexico ■ Steven Bell, **Universidad la Salle**, Mexico City, Mexico ■ Damian Benstead, **Sungkyunkwan University**, Seoul, Korea ■ Paul Cameron, **National Chengchi University**, Taipei, Taiwan R.O.C. ■ Sun Chang, **Soongsil University**, Seoul, Korea ■ Grace Chao, **Soochow University**, Taipei, Taiwan R.O.C. ■ Chien Ping Chen, **Hua Fan University**, Taipei, Taiwan R.O.C. ■ Selma Chen, **Chihlee Institute of Technology**, Taipei, Taiwan R.O.C. ■ Sylvia Chiu, **Soochow University**, Taipei, Taiwan R.O.C. ■ Mary Colonna, **Columbia University**, New York, New York ■ Lee Culver, **Miami-Dade Community College,** Miami, Florida ■ Joy Durighello, **City College of San Francisco**, San Francisco, California ■ Isabel Del Valle, **ULATINA**, San Jose, Costa Rica ■ Linda Emerson, **Sogang University**, Seoul, Korea ■ Esther Entin, **Miami-Dade Community College**, Miami, Florida ■ Glenn Farrier, **Gakushuin Women's College**, Tokyo, Japan ■ Su Wei Feng, Taipei, Taiwan R.O.C. ■ Judith Garcia, **Miami-Dade Community College**, Miami, Florida ■ Maxine Gillway, **United Arab Emirates University**, Al Ain, United Arab Emirates ■ Colin Gullberg, **Soochow University**, Taipei, Taiwan R.O.C. ■ Natasha Haugnes, **Academy of Art University**, San Francisco, California ■ Barbara Hockman, **City College of San Francisco**, San Francisco, California ■ Jinyoung Hong, **Sogang University**, Seoul, Korea ■ Sherry Hsieh, **Christ's College**, Taipei, Taiwan R.O.C. ■ Yu-shen Hsu, **Soochow University**, Taipei, Taiwan R.O.C. ■ Cheung Kai-Chong, **Shih-Shin University**, Taipei, Taiwan R.O.C. ■ Leslie Kanberg, **City College of San Francisco**, San Francisco, California ■ Gregory Keech, **City College of San Francisco**, San Francisco, California ■ Susan Kelly, **Sogang University**, Seoul, Korea ■ Myoungsuk Kim, **Soongsil University**, Seoul, Korea ■ Youngsuk Kim, **Soongsil University**, Seoul, Korea ■ Roy Langdon, **Sungkyunkwan University**, Seoul, Korea ■ Rocio Lara, **University of Costa Rica**, San Jose, Costa Rica ■ Insung Lee, **Soongsil University**, Seoul, Korea ■ Andy Leung, **National Tsing Hua University**, Taipei, Taiwan R.O.C. ■ Elisa Li Chan, **University of Costa Rica**, San Jose, Costa Rica ■ Elizabeth Lorenzo, **Universidad Internacional de las Americas**, San Jose, Costa Rica ■ Cheryl Magnant, **Sungkyunkwan University**, Seoul, Korea ■ Narciso Maldonado Iuit, **Escuela Tecnica Electricista**, Mexico City, Mexico ■ Shaun Manning, **Hankuk University of Foreign Studies**, Seoul, Korea ■ Yoshiko Matsubayashi, **Tokyo International University**, Saitama, Japan ■ Scott Miles, **Sogang University**, Seoul, Korea ■ William Mooney, **Chinese Culture University**, Taipei, Taiwan R.O.C. ■ Jeff Moore, **Sungkyunkwan University**, Seoul, Korea ■ Mavelin de Moreno, **Lehnsen Roosevelt School**, Guatemala City, Guatemala ■ Ahmed Motala, **University of Sharjah**, Sharjah, United Arab Emirates ■ Carlos Navarro, **University of Costa Rica**, San Jose, Costa Rica ■ Dan Neal, **Chih Chien University**, Taipei, Taiwan R.O.C. ■ Margarita Novo, **University of Costa Rica**, San Jose, Costa Rica ■ Karen O'Neill, **San Jose State University**, San Jose, California ■ Linda O'Roke, **City College of San Francisco**, San Francisco, California ■ Martha Padilla, **Colegio de Bachilleres de Sinaloa,** Culiacan, Mexico ■ Allen Quesada, **University of Costa Rica**, San Jose, Costa Rica ■ Jim Rogge, **Broward Community College**, Ft. Lauderdale, Florida ■ Marge Ryder, **City College of San Francisco**, San Francisco, California ■ Gerardo Salas, **University of Costa Rica**, San Jose, Costa Rica ■ Shigeo Sato, **Tamagawa University**, Tokyo, Japan ■ Lynn Schneider, **City College of San Francisco**, San Francisco, California ■ Devan Scoble, **Sungkyunkwan University**, Seoul, Korea ■ Maryjane Scott, **Soongsil University**, Seoul, Korea ■ Ghaida Shaban, **Makassed Philanthropic School**, Beirut, Lebanon ■ Maha Shalok, **Makassed Philanthropic School**, Beirut, Lebanon ■ John Shannon, **University of Sharjah**, Sharjah, United Arab Emirates ■ Elsa Sheng, **National Technology College of Taipei**, Taipei, Taiwan R.O.C. ■ Ye-Wei Sheng, **National Taipei College of Business**, Taipei, Taiwan R.O.C. ■ Emilia Sobaja, **University of Costa Rica**, San Jose, Costa Rica ■ You-Souk Yoon, **Sungkyunkwan University**, Seoul, Korea ■ Shanda Stromfield, **San Jose State University**, San Jose, California ■ Richard Swingle, **Kansai Gaidai College**, Osaka, Japan ■ Carol Sung, **Christ's College**, Taipei, Taiwan R.O.C. ■ Jeng-Yih Tim Hsu, **National Kaohsiung First University of Science and Technology**, Kaohsiung, Taiwan R.O.C. ■ Shinichiro Torikai, **Rikkyo University**, Tokyo, Japan ■ Sungsoon Wang, **Sogang University**, Seoul, Korea ■ Kathleen Wolf, **City College of San Francisco**, San Francisco, California ■ Sean Wray, **Waseda University International**, Tokyo, Japan ■ Belinda Yanda, **Academy of Art University**, San Francisco, California ■ Su Huei Yang, **National Taipei College of Business**, Taipei, Taiwan R.O.C. ■ Tzu Yun Yu, **Chungyu Institute of Technology**, Taipei, Taiwan R.O.C.

Photo Credits for Interactions 2 Writing ©2007

Page 3: © BananaStock/JupiterImages; 4: © David Young Wolff/PhotoEdit; 8, 9: © Comstock Images/JupiterImages; 16: © Bob Daemmrich/The Image Works; 23: © Royalty-Free/ CORBIS; 24 (left): © Thomas Hartwell/CORBIS; 25 (right): © SuperStock, Inc./SuperStock; 27 (left): © D. Normark/PhotoLink/Getty Images; 27 (right): © Andrew Ward/Life File/Getty Images; 31: © Rainer Hackenberg/VISUM/The Image Works; 35: © Robert A. Isaacs/Photo Researchers; 39: © Digital Vision Ltd; 40: © Scenics of America/PhotoLink/Getty Images; 43: © PhotoLink/Getty Images; 49: © Comstock Images/JupiterImages; 59: © John Fung; 65: © Royalty-Free/CORBIS; 68: © RubberBall Productions/Getty Images; 72: © Big Cheese Photo/JupiterImages; 73: © Digital Vision; 80: © Stockbyte/Punchstock Images; 85: © Rafa Rivas/AFP/Getty Images: 89: © Colin Garratt, Milepost 92 1/2/CORBIS; 101: © Ryan McVay/ Getty Images; 102: AP/Wide World Photos; 103 (top left and bottom): © Digital Vision/Getty Images; 103 (top right): © Lucos/The Image Worls; 108: © Dr. Parvinder Sethi; 110: © Reuters/CORBIS; 117: © Comstock/PictureQuest; 118: © Robin Nelson/Zuma/Corbis; 124: © Barbara Penoyar /Getty Images; 128: © John Fung; 130: © Marc Garanger/CORBIS; 131: © Barbara Penoyar/Getty Images; 137: © Comstock/SuperStock; 138 (top left): © Royalty-Free/CORBIS; 138 (top right): © BananaStock/JupiterImages; 138 (bottom): © John Fung; 143: © Peter Hvizdak/The Image Works; 149: © Mark Richards/PhotoEdit; 151: © Justin Sullivan/Getty Images; 157: © NASA/Getty Images; 166: © PhotoLink/Getty Images; 168, 179: © Royalty-Free/CORBIS; 181: © PhotoDisc/Getty Images; 182: © World Religions Photo Library/Alamy; 185: © Comstock Images/JupiterImages; 191: © Buccina Studios/Getty Images; 193: © Jack Hollingsworth/Getty Images; 194: © PhotoLink/Getty Images.

***Interactions/Mosaic* Silver Edition** is a fully-integrated, 18-book academic skills series. Language proficiencies are articulated from the beginning through advanced levels within each of the four language skill strands. Chapter themes articulate across the four skill strands to systematically recycle content, vocabulary, and grammar.

NEW to the Silver Edition:

- **World's most popular and comprehensive academic skills series**—thoroughly updated for today's global learners
- **New design** showcases compelling instructional photos to strengthen the educational experience
- **Enhanced focus on vocabulary building, test taking, and critical thinking skills** promotes academic achievement
- **New strategies and activities for the TOEFL® iBT** build invaluable test taking skills
- **New "Best Practices" approach** promotes excellence in language teaching

NEW to Interactions 2 Writing:

- **All new content:**—Chapter 10 Ceremonies
- **Transparent chapter structure** with consistent part headings, activity labeling, and clear guidance—strengthens the academic experience:

  Part 1: Before You Write
  Part 2: Developing Writing Skills
  Part 3: Revising and Editing
  Part 4: Expansion Activities

- **Writing Articulation Chart** (inside back cover) shows how the four Writing books lead students from successful sentence building to effective academic essay writing
- **Systematically structured, multi-step *Writing Process*** culminates in a *Writing Product* task
- **Step-by-step paragraph revision process** leads students from focusing on big-picture issues (*Revising*) to reviewing word- and sentence-level concerns (*Editing*)
- **New and direct connections between writing and grammar** tie the writing skill in focus with the grammar structures needed to develop each writing skill
- **New communicative activities** invite students to interact meaningfully with target words to build vocabulary skills for writing
- **New self-evaluation rubric** for each chapter supports the learner as he or she builds confidence and autonomy in academic writing

---

* TOEFL is a registered trademark of Educational Testing Service (ETS). This publication is not endorsed or approved by ETS.

Our Interactions/Mosaic Silver Edition team has produced an edition that focuses on Best Practices, principles that contribute to excellent language teaching and learning. Our team of writers, editors, and teacher consultants has identified the following six interconnected Best Practices:

Making Use of Academic Content

Materials and tasks based on academic content and experiences give learning real purpose. Students explore real world issues, discuss academic topics, and study content-based and thematic materials.

Organizing Information

Students learn to organize thoughts and notes through a variety of graphic organizers that accommodate diverse learning and thinking styles.

Scaffolding Instruction

A scaffold is a physical structure that facilitates construction of a building. Similarly, scaffolding instruction is a tool used to facilitate language learning in the form of predictable and flexible tasks. Some examples include oral or written modeling by the teacher or students, placing information in a larger framework, and reinterpretation.

Activating Prior Knowledge

Students can better understand new spoken or written material when they connect to the content. Activating prior knowledge allows students to tap into what they already know, building on this knowledge, and stirring a curiosity for more knowledge.

Interacting with Others

Activities that promote human interaction in pair work, small group work, and whole class activities present opportunities for real world contact and real world use of language.

Cultivating Critical Thinking

Strategies for critical thinking are taught explicitly. Students learn tools that promote critical thinking skills crucial to success in the academic world.

Making Use of Academic Content
Academic themes, activities, and writing topics prepare students for university life.

New design showcases compelling instructional photos to strengthen the educational experience.

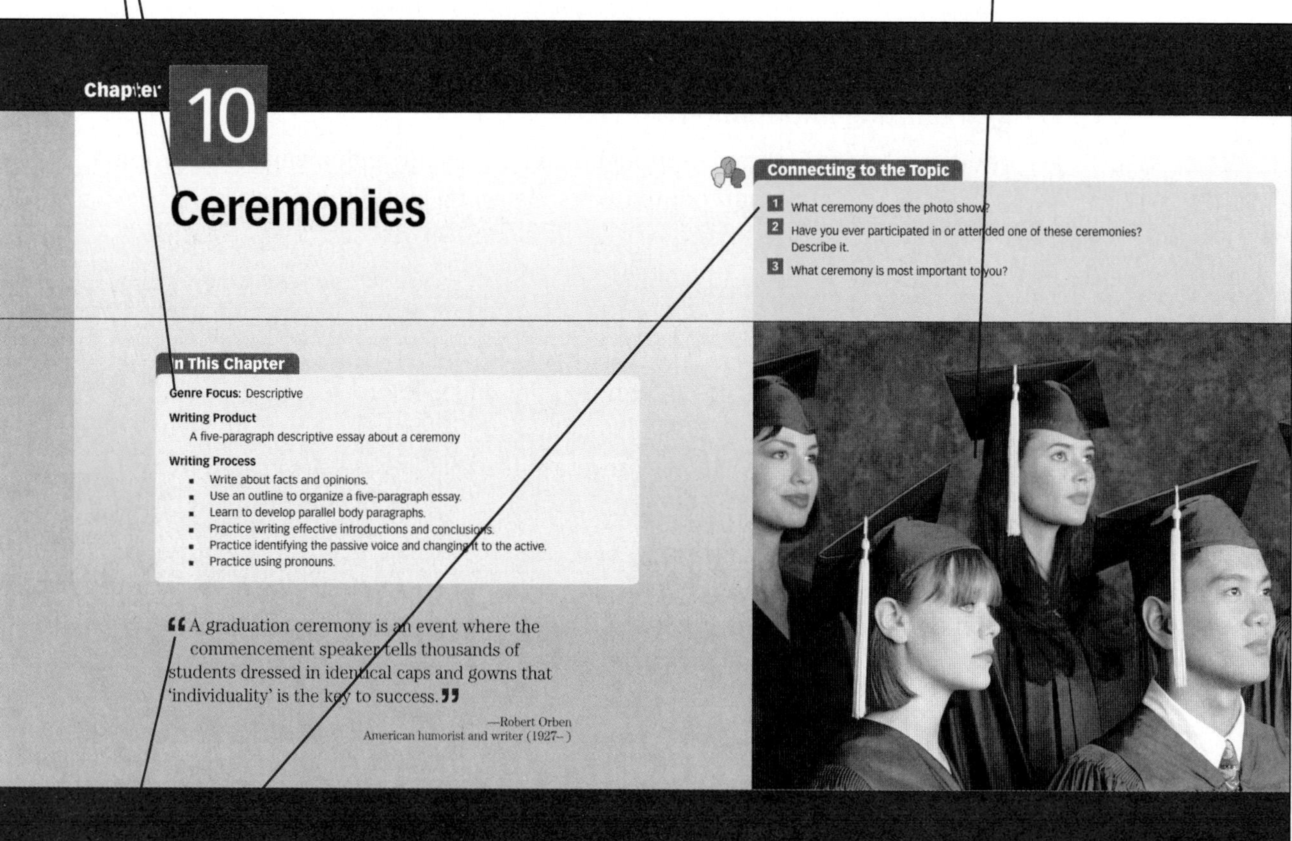

Interacting with Others
Questions and topical quotes stimulate interest, activate prior knowledge, and launch the topic of the unit.

Activating Prior Knowledge
Chapter opening questions and pre-writing discussions activate prior knowledge and create a foundation for the writing activity.

Cultivating Critical Thinking
Critical thinking strategies and activities equip students with the skills they need for academic achievement.

Part 1 Before You Write

Exploring Ideas

1 Describing Scenes Look at the photos of streets below, and choose one of them to describe. Write as much as you can in 10 minutes. Answer the following questions:

1. What is happening on the street?
2. Would you like to live in this neighborhood? Why or why not?
3. How is the street similar to or different from the street where you live?

▲ A street in Cairo

▲ A street in Berlin

2 Sharing Your Ideas Form a small group with other students who wrote about the same photo you did. Share and discuss what you wrote. Did you notice the same things in the photo? Did you have the same opinion of the scene?

Strategy

Writing About Sense Details and Feelings
In this chapter you are going to write a descriptive paragraph about where you live: your neighborhood, your street, your dormitory, your apartment or house, or your room. A good description includes *sense details*: the things you can see, hear, touch, taste, and smell.

What Do You Think?

Classifying Sense Details
Work with a partner, and test your knowledge of the adjectives below. Put each adjective in the correct category. (Note: Some might fit into more than one category.) Then add some adjectives of your own to each category.

bitter	cramped	noisy	salty	smooth
bright	foul	rotten	soft	spicy
colorful	gloomy	rough	sour	

See	Hear	Smell	Taste	Touch
	noisy			

3 Choosing a Topic Write the name of the place you are going to describe in your descriptive paragraph.

4 Listing Details Make a list of sense details for the place you are going to describe. Use noun phrases and adjectives.

1. What I can see:
   colorful piles of vegetables
   ______
2. What I can hear:
   ______
3. What I can touch:
   ______
4. What I can taste (optional):
   ______
5. What I can smell (optional):
   ______

Scaffolding Instruction

Instruction and practice with sentence and paragraph skills help build a solid foundation for essay writing.

Organizing Information

Graphic organizers provide tools for organizing information and ideas.

Organizing Ideas

Strategy

Writing Topic Sentences

The topic sentence tells the reader the subject of the paragraph. In a descriptive paragraph, the topic sentence is general enough to unite all the descriptive details in the paragraph but focused enough to grab the reader's attention. It should also indicate the writer's feeling about the place.

Instead of using vague, overused adjectives such as *nice, good,* and *bad* in your topic sentences, use more specific and vivid adjectives.

Vague and uninteresting: My neighborhood is a nice place to live.
Specific and interesting: My neighborhood is fascinating because people from many countries live in it.

10 Choosing the Best Topic Sentence For each set of topic sentences below, put a check mark (✔) next to the best topic sentence, the one that is focused and interesting.

1. Topic: "My Room"
   - a. _____ My room is a perfect place for one person to live.
   - b. _____ Many people live in single rooms.
   - c. _____ My room is nice.
   - d. _____ I love the big windows.
2. Topic: "My House"
   - a. _____ There are a lot of houses like mine in my neighborhood.
   - b. _____ I love my house because it is filled with happy memories.
   - c. _____ Big houses are best.
   - d. _____ My family lives in a good house.
3. Topic: "My Dormitory"
   - a. _____ My dormitory has never felt like home to me.
   - b. _____ I live in a dormitory.
   - c. _____ Dormitories are where students live.
   - d. _____ The cafeteria food in my dormitory is good.

11 Writing and Sharing a Draft Topic Sentence Write a draft topic sentence for your own descriptive paragraph. Then in small groups, discuss each other's topic sentences. Answer the following questions:

1. Does the topic sentence introduce the place to be described?
2. Does it grab the reader's attention?
3. Does it indicate the writer's feeling about the place?

Using Graphic Organizers

Strategy

Using a Graphic Organizer to Organize Details for a Paragraph

One way to brainstorm and organize ideas for a focused descriptive paragraph is to use a graphic organizer. Graphic organizers show how ideas are connected to each other.

The graphic organizer below is called a *mind map*. In the mind map, the topic sentence is in the center. The main supporting details are connected directly to the topic sentence. The secondary details are connected to the main details.

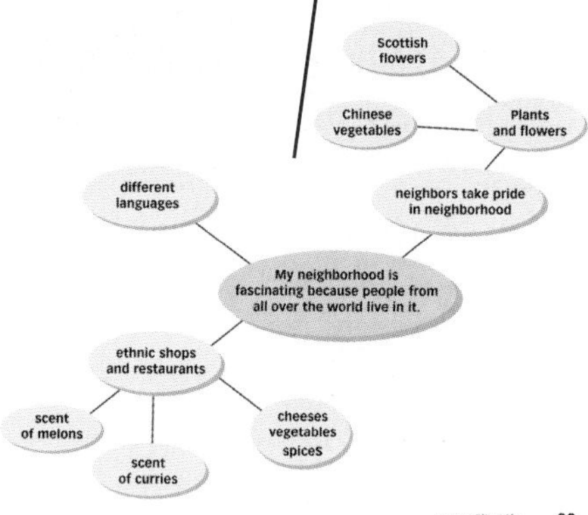

Enhanced focus on vocabulary building promotes academic achievement.

New strategies and activities for the TOEFL® iBT build invaluable test taking skills.

Building Vocabulary

5 Matching Words to Their Definitions In the web page article on page 45, underline the words listed below. Use the context to help you guess the meaning. Then match the words with their meanings.

1. _h_ armored — a. very happy
2. ___ split — b. pick up
3. ___ spew — c. charge with a crime
4. ___ recover — d. tear open
5. ___ scoop up — e. find
6. ___ gleeful — f. spill
7. ___ bonanza — g. sudden riches
8. ___ prosecute — h. protected with strong metal
9. ___ convict — i. find guilty of a crime
10. ___ insured — j. protected from loss

6 Using a Vocabulary Chart In your letter to the editor, you might want to use some of the words above. First put each of them in the correct column below. Then write sentences with five of the words, giving your opinion of the happenings in the article.

Noun	Verbs	Adjectizes
		insured

E ample

Even though the money was insured, the drivers shouldn t have taken it

Strategy

Writing a Conclusion

The final paragraph of an essay is the conclusion. The conclusion usually sums up what was said in the body of the paragraph and includes an additional thought or personal opinion on the topic. The conclusion should not go off topic or introduce new ideas.

15 Analy ing a Conclusion Look at the conclusion to the essay in Activity 12. Which part summarizes what was said in the body paragraph? Which part adds new thoughts or opinions?

16 Preparing to Write a Conclusion Write notes for a conclusion for your essay.

TOEFL® IBT **Focus on Testing**

Organi ing Information Before You Write

In this chapter, you practiced listing similarities and differences between living situations. It is often helpful to make this kind of list before you start writing a response on a timed writing test. However, tests like the TOEFL Internet-Based Test (iBT) usually ask you to focus specifically on differences.

The best way to plan a timed response to a question about differences is to make a table with two lists side-by-side. Each list is for one side of an issue. For example, if the prompt asks, "How do Dr. Smith's views about living situations differ from Professor Baker's?" you would make one list for Dr. Smith's views and, right beside it, another for Professor Baker's views. Read the information in the following contrast table.

Contrast Table

Prof. Baker's Views (in support of lizing alone)	Dr. Smith's Views (in support of lizing with others)
College students who live with other people get better grades in the humanities and social sciences than those who live alone.	College students who live alone get better grades in mathematics than those living with other people.
Students who live alone do not spend enough time interacting with others.	Students who live with others do not spend enough time studying.
When you live by yourself, you might let your apartment get so dirty that it is bad for your health.	When you live with other people, you have to clean the house regularly, which is a waste of time.

Chapter	Writing Product	Idea Development/ Organizing Skills	Revising and Editing
1 Education and Student Life page 2	An **opinion** paragraph about large and small colleges	Organizing ideas in order of importance Supporting opinions with reasons Writing topic sentences	Revising for content: topic sentence and support for opinions Editing for form: paragraph format
2 City Life page 22	A **descriptive** paragraph about where you live	Writing topic sentences and concluding sentences for descriptive paragraphs Using a mind map to organize information Eliminating irrelevant details	Revising for content: relevance of details Editing for form: comma splices
3 Business and Money page 42	An **argument** letter in response to a web page article.	Free writing to generate ideas Using a graphic organizer to connect arguments and reasons Analyzing the organization of a letter	Revising for content: faulty reasoning Editing for form: hyphenation errors

Critical Thinking	Grammar	Vocabulary Building	Focus on Testing
Ranking factors Using reasons to support opinions Identifying and correcting overgeneralizations	Giving reasons with *because*, *so*, and *therefore* Listing reasons with *first of all*, *finally*, *in addition*, and *also* Making generalizations with present tense verbs	Generating vocabulary through discussion Developing vocabulary in a semantic field: academic environments	TOEFL® IBT General statements on standardized tests
Classifying sense details Evaluating the relevance of information	Giving reasons with *since* Varying sentence structure in a paragraph Identifying dependent clauses	Using context to define words Developing vocabulary in a semantic field: sense details	TOEFL® IBT Brainstorming for Ideas
Identifying and avoiding faulty reasoning Supporting an opinion with examples and predictions	Expressing obligation with *must*, *have to*, and *should*	Using context to define words Identifying parts of speech	TOEFL® IBT Stating a specific point of view

Chapter	Writing Product	Idea Development/ Organizing Skills	Revising and Editing
4 Jobs and Professions page 64	A one-paragraph personal **narrative**	Using a spider map to organize ideas Dividing information into two paragraphs Stating things directly and implying them Limiting information	Revising for content: relevance and cohesion Editing for form: capitalization and verb forms
5 Lifestyles Around the World page 84	A two-paragraph personal **narrative**	Using a graphic organizer to plan a narrative Dividing a narrative into two paragraphs Identifying omissions and digressions	Revising for Content: digressions Editing for Form: verb forms
6 Global Connections page 100	Two **argument** paragraphs for or against globalization	Using examples to define a broad term Using a clustergram to organize information for an argument Writing a topic sentence for argument paragraphs	Revising for content: combining sentences Editing for form: punctuating relative clauses

Critical Thinking	Grammar	Vocabulary Building	Focus on Testing
Evaluating accom-plishments Determining ways to imply personal qualities Assessing writing progress	Using the simple past and present perfect tenses Using the present perfect continuous Using demonstratives	Developing vocabulary with antonyms Using an online dictionary Developing vocabulary in a semantic field: personal characteristics	TOEFL® IBT Reviewing writing for the correct verb tense
Analyzing the moral of a story Evaluating a writer's decisions	Using the past perfect tense Choosing the correct verb form	Developing vocabulary in a semantic field: life lessons Using a thesaurus	TOEFL® IBT Using personal anecdotes on writing exams
Evaluating globalization Supporting an argument with examples Evaluating Internet sources Choosing the best argument	Using the correct form of a word Using relative clauses	Developing vocabulary in a semantic field: globalization Analyzing word parts	TOEFL® IBT Using graphic organizers for written exams

Chapter	Writing Product	Idea Development/ Organizing Skills	Revising and Editing
7 Language and Communication page 116	A **narrative** essay about a classmate	Focusing on one subject Writing introductory and concluding paragraphs Organizing information in a three-paragraph essay	Revising for content: introductions, conclusions, and digressions Editing for form: punctuation with transition words and subordinators
8 Tastes and Preferences page 136	A **comparative** essay about two types of housing	Free writing to develop ideas Using a comparison chart to organize ideas Analyzing the structure of an essay Writing introductions and conclusions	Revising for content: transition words Editing for form: comparative and superlative forms
9 New Frontiers page 156	A **descriptive** essay about a planet	Getting information from charts and tables Using an idea map to organize information Ordering information within sub-topics Analyzing the structure of an essay	Revising for content: incorporating new information Editing for form: form of passive voice
10 Ceremonies page 178	A five-paragraph **descriptive** essay about a ceremony	Free writing to develop ideas Using an outline to organize a five-paragraph essay Analyzing the structure of an essay	Revising for content: organization and completeness Editing for form: form of passive and active voice

Critical Thinking	Grammar	Vocabulary Building	Focus on Testing
Identifying reasons for immigration Evaluating questions for appropriateness Classifying emotions	Using gerund subjects Using *would* and *used to* Identifying and correcting parallelism problems	Developing vocabulary in a semantic field: emotions Using *–ed* and *–ing* adjectives	TOEFL® IBT Using *wh*-questions to develop ideas
Finding bases of comparison Categorizing nouns Analyzing word parts	Using *both* and *neither* Using comparatives and superlatives Using *while*, *in contrast*, and *on the other hand*	Developing vocabulary in a semantic field: housing Using antonyms to generate new vocabulary Analyzing word parts	TOEFL® IBT Organizing information before you write
Speculating about a topic Analyzing the organization of an essay	Using the passive voice Varying sentence structure with *with* and *unlike* + noun phrase Giving reasons with *because* and *because of*	Developing vocabulary in a semantic field: space Using suffixes to guess the meaning of new words	TOEFL® IBT Writing descriptions
Distinguishing facts and opinions Evaluating an Outline	Avoiding the passive voice Using pronouns to unify paragraphs	Developing vocabulary in a semantic field: ceremonies and rites of passage Using word families to develop vocabulary	TOEFL® IBT Making connections between readings and lectures

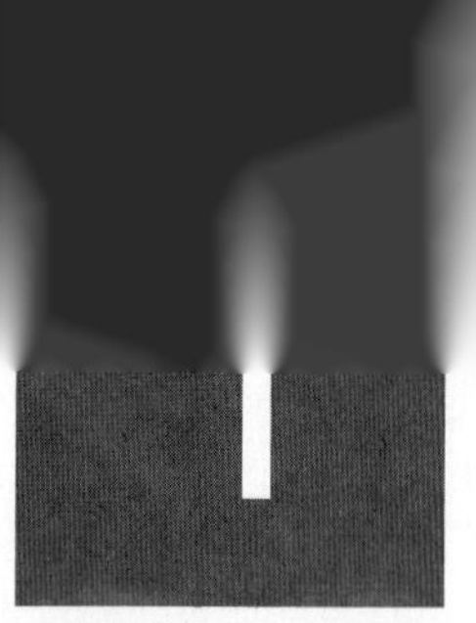

Education and Student Life

In This Chapter

Genre Focus: Argument

Writing Product

An opinion paragraph about large and small colleges

Writing Process

- Rank decision-making factors in order of importance.
- Organize ideas in order of importance.
- Write a topic sentence for an opinion paragraph.
- Give reasons with *because, so,* and *therefore.*
- Connect ideas with *first of all, finally, in addition,* and *also.*
- Make general statements.
- Avoid overgeneralizations.
- Use a writing rubric to evaluate a first draft.

"The direction in which education starts a man will determine his future life."

—Plato
Greek philosopher (428–347 BC)

Connecting to the Topic

1. Have you ever attended a class like this?
2. What would the advantages be of a class like this?
3. Would there be any disadvantages? If so, what?

Part 1 Before You Write

Exploring Ideas

▲ There are many types of books and brochures about different colleges.

What Do You Think?

Ranking Factors

Below are some factors a student might think about when choosing a college. Which ones are most important to you? Rank them in order from 1 (most important) to 12 (least important).

_____ class size
_____ facilities (libraries, laboratories)
_____ location
_____ quality of classes
_____ number of international students
_____ special programs
_____ courses offered
_____ cost
_____ ease of admission
_____ prestige
_____ help with job placement
_____ family connection

1 Adding Factors Think about the factors listed above. Are there any other factors you would add? Write them on a separate piece of paper.

2 Discussing Your Ideas In small groups, discuss your ideas with other students. Give reasons you think certain factors are important.

Building Vocabulary

3 Using a Vocabulary Chart Look at the vocabulary words in the chart below. Look up any words you don't understand. Circle the words used in your discussion in Activity 2, and add words to the list. Then continue the discussion using any words on the list that you have not yet used.

Nouns	Verbs	Adjectives	Other
advantage	attend	advantageous	
attendance	prefer	challenging	
campus		diverse	
disadvantage		huge	
facility		impersonal	
faculty		prestigious	
location			
preference			
prestige			
scholarship			
student body			
tuition			

4 Matching Words to Their Definitions Match the vocabulary words in Activity 3 with the words and phrases below.

1. a good thing ___advantage___
2. the cost of college classes ________
3. very large ________
4. a good reputation ________
5. teachers ________
6. a building, a laboratory, a library ________
7. go to ________
8. having many different kinds ________
9. not friendly ________
10. a bad thing ________

5 Discussing Advantages In small groups, discuss the advantages of large and small colleges. Write your ideas on the lines below.

Advantages of a Large College

____

____

____

____

____

____

Advantages of a Small College

____

____

____

____

____

____

6 Discussing Preferences Look at your lists of advantages. In small groups, discuss whether you think large or small colleges are better.

7 Choosing a Topic Choose the topic you want to write about: the advantages of a large college or the advantages of a small college.

Organizing Ideas

Strategy

Organizing Ideas in Order of Importance

When you made the list of the advantages of large and small colleges, you were giving your opinion. Once you have decided on your opinions, you need to organize them. One way of doing this is to write about the most important ideas first, then write about the less important ones.

8 Ranking Ideas in Order of Importance Look at the lists of advantages you made in Activity 5. Which advantages are most important to you? Rank these advantages in order of importance, with the first one as the most important. Cross out any advantages that are not very important.

Strategy

Giving Reasons

When you write, you should give at least one reason or example to support each of your opinions. You need to tell your readers what you think and why you think it.

9 **Giving Reasons for Your Opinions** On the following lines, list your opinions about the advantages of small or large colleges in order of importance. Then give at least one reason or example for each opinion. This will make an outline you can use when you write.

Opinion 1: *It's easier to make a lot of friends at a small college.* ______

Reason: *If there are fewer students, you see the same people more often and get to know them better.*

Opinion 2: ______________________________

Reason: ______________________________

Opinion 3: ______________________________

Reason: ______________________________

Opinion 4: ______________________________

Reason: ______________________________

Strategy

Writing Topic Sentences

The topic sentence usually comes at the beginning of a paragraph. It tells the reader the main idea of the paragraph. A good topic sentence shouldn't be too specific because it needs to relate to all the ideas in the paragraph. In addition, in an opinion paragraph, a good topic sentence will clearly state your opinion.

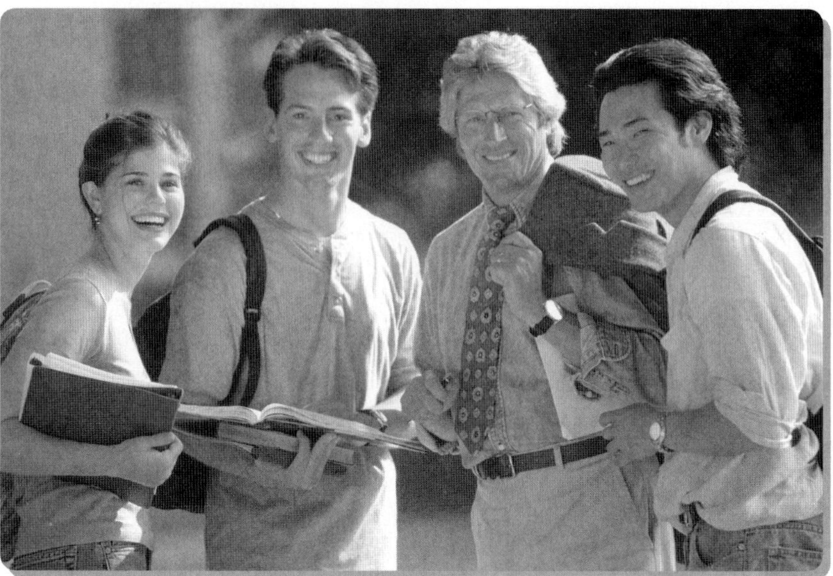

▲ Studying in a foreign country can be fun.

10 Choosing the Best Topic Sentence Look at the list of possible topic sentences for an opinion paragraph about the advantages of studying abroad. Discuss them in groups or as a class. In your opinion, which topic sentences will work? Which ones won't? Why?

1. Students who study abroad often can't speak the language well.
2. Studying abroad has three main advantages.
3. I believe this for several reasons.
4. There are many good schools in foreign countries.
5. If possible, all college students should spend some time studying in a foreign country.

11 Writing a Draft Topic Sentence Write a draft topic sentence for your paragraph about the advantages of large or small colleges.

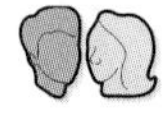

12 Sharing Your Topic Sentence Work with a partner. Read each other's topic sentences. Give your partner feedback by answering the following questions about his or her topic sentence:

1. Is it a complete sentence?
2. Does it tell the reader what the author is going to write about?
3. Is it too general or too specific?
4. Does it include the author's opinion?

Part 2 Developing Writing Skills

Developing Cohesion and Clarity

GIVING REASONS WITH *BECAUSE*, *SO*, AND *THEREFORE*

When you give reasons to support your opinions, you may want to use connectors that show cause or result. Note the different punctuation and capitalization in sentences with these three connectors.

Use *because* in phrases and clauses that state a cause or reason.

Examples

Because large schools offer many different courses, students have a wide variety of subjects to choose from.

Students at large schools have a wide variety of subjects to choose from because large schools offer many different courses.

Use *so* and *therefore* in phrases and clauses that state an effect or result.

Examples

Large schools offer many different courses, so students have a wide variety of subjects to choose from.

Large schools offer many different courses; therefore, students have a wide variety of subjects to choose from.

Large schools offer many different courses. Therefore, students have a wide variety of subjects to choose from.

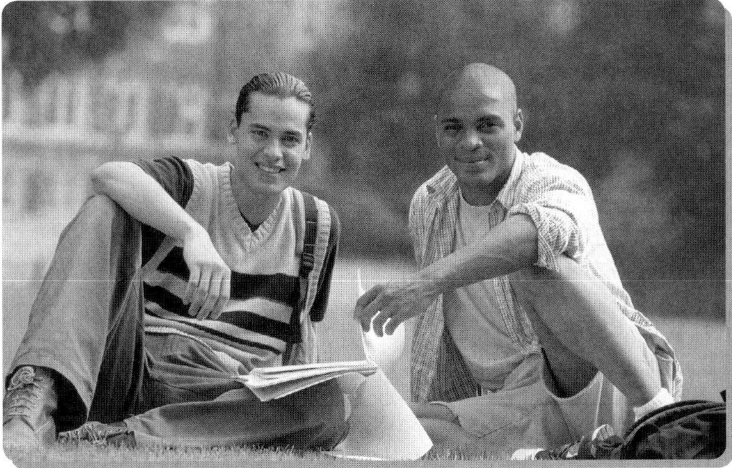

▲ Large universities and small colleges can both offer diversity.

1 Completing Sentences with *Because*, *So*, and *Therefore*

Complete the following sentences with *because*, *so*, or *therefore*.

1. Students who study in a foreign country live with people who do not speak their native language; therefore, they will learn that country's language well.
2. Public colleges are more practical ____________ they are less expensive.
3. When students attend a local college, they can live at home, ____________ they don't have to spend a lot on rent and food.
4. ____________ international students have to study in a foreign language, they often have difficulty with their courses.
5. International students spend a long time away from home. ____________, they may lose touch with their own customs and culture.

USING CONNECTING WORDS: *IN ADDITION* AND *ALSO*

In a paragraph, it's important to use connecting words—words that connect the ideas. Otherwise, the paragraph will sound choppy—that is, not smooth. You can make a paragraph more cohesive by using *in addition* and *also* to connect similar ideas.

In addition usually comes at the beginning of a sentence. In this position, it is always followed by a comma.

Example

It is very difficult to study abroad. In addition, it can be much more expensive than studying in your own country.

Also can come at the beginning of a sentence, before a simple present or a past tense verb, or after an auxiliary verb or modal. Note that if it comes at the beginning of a sentence, it is followed by a comma.

Examples

Also, large universities offer a more diverse student population.
Large universities also offer a more diverse student population.
Large universities can also offer a more diverse student population.

---

2 Connecting Sentences with *Also* and *In Addition*

Use *also* and *in addition* to connect the sentences. More than one answer is possible.

1. Many students learn a lot about the world from their study abroad experience. They learn a lot about themselves.

   Many students learn a lot about the world from their study abroad experience. They also learn a lot about themselves.

   ____

2. Most students in four-year colleges are very intelligent. They study hard.

____

____

____

3. Some professors don't always understand international students. They may know very little about foreign cultures.

____

____

____

4. Many students who go abroad to study lose contact with their families. Some of them marry foreigners and never return home.

____

____

____

5. Studying in a foreign country can be more exciting than studying in your native country. You may get a better education.

____

____

____

3 Rewriting a Paragraph with Connecting Words Rewrite the following paragraph using *also* and *in addition* to connect similar ideas.

Studying abroad offers students many advantages. First of all, students have the opportunity to learn a new language by interacting with native speakers every day. The students live in a new culture, so they can learn both in and out of the classroom. Studying abroad teaches students that there are other ways of looking at the world. This is a very important part of education. Students learn to be flexible because they have to adapt to different ways of living. They experience another culture in a much more significant way than if they simply took a vacation to another country. Foreign students are far from home. Therefore, they have to become responsible and self-reliant. When they study abroad, students have an experience they will remember all their lives.

USING TRANSITION WORDS AND PHRASES: *FIRST OF ALL* AND *FINALLY*

Use *first of all* and *finally* when you want to list several points. *First of all* starts the list, and *finally* ends it. These are also called *listing cues.*

Examples

> There are many reasons international students might feel homesick. First of all, they may be away from their families for the first time. In addition, there is the problem of adapting to a completely different culture. Finally, not knowing the native language can make students feel isolated.

Note that *first of all* and *finally* come at the beginning of a sentence and are always followed by a comma.

4 Writing Sentences with *First of All* and *Finally* Look at your notes for your paragraph. Are there any ideas that you want to list? Write those ideas using *first of all* and *finally.*

MAKING GENERAL STATEMENTS WITH PRESENT TENSE VERBS

There are several ways to make statements that are generally true. Look at the sentences in the activities in this chapter and answer these questions:

1. What tense are the verbs?
2. Are the subjects usually singular or plural?
3. Does the article usually precede the subject?

You will notice that general statements are in the simple present tense and that the subjects are usually plural with no articles. When the subjects are people, singular personal pronouns can be awkward in English. For example, look at the following sentences. Which sentence sounds awkward? Why?

Students must leave their families.
A student must leave his or her family.

When you write sentences that contain general statements, make sure you follow these rules:

1. Use simple present verbs.
2. Add -*s* to verbs with third-person singular subjects (*he*, *she,* or *it*).
3. Count nouns should generally be plural with no article.
4. Pronouns must agree in number with their antecedents.

The sentence, *Every student should try to hold on to his or her culture,* is correct although it is awkward.

The sentence, *Every student should try to hold on to their culture,* is incorrect because *student* is singular and *their* is plural.

---

5 **Finding and Correcting Mistakes** Find the mistakes in the underlined words in the sentences below. Make corrections based on the four rules on page 12, or write *correct* above the correct sentences.

1. Most ~~family~~ *families* save for many years to send their children to college.
2. Some students feel homesick.
3. Some small schools don't have good library.
4. A large school has fewer teachers on their faculty.
5. A school with many courses offer more majors.
6. People who work often prefer to attend community colleges.

TOEFL® IBT

Focus on Testing

General Statements on Standardized Tests

A prompt is a set of directions for a question on a writing test. On the TOEFL®Internet-Based Test (iBT), there are two types of writing prompts. One is for a 20-minute "integrated" writing task. The other is for a 30-minute "independent" writing task. Here are some sample prompts for the independent task:

Sample 1 *Students should work for at least one year after high school before entering college.*

Do you agree with this statement? Discuss reasons for your opinion with a partner. Support your opinions with specific examples.

Sample 2 *Socializing is having conversations, going to parties, or doing any recreational activity with other people.*

Do you prefer to socialize with other students or with nonstudents? Explain your preference to your partner, and give specific examples to support it.

In this chapter, you learned that the simple present tense is very effective for making general statements. The sample prompts above use the simple present tense.

Practice To practice writing general statements in response to TOEFL® iBT writing prompts, add more general statements to each list in the chart on the next page. Each list relates to one of the sample prompts.

Sample Prompt 1: Working Before College	Sample Prompt 2: Socializing with Students or Nonstudents
Working can help you decide what you want to study.	Socializing with nonstudents gives you a better sense of the town or city where you are studying.

Strategy

Avoiding Overgeneralizations

When you write, it is important to not overgeneralize; that is, do not make statements that are so general that they are not true.

Examples of overgeneralizations

All international students work harder than other students. (This is not always true.)

Teenagers are always irresponsible. (This is not always true.)

To avoid overgeneralizations:

Don't use the adverbs of frequency, *never* or *always,* when you are giving your opinion about something.

Instead of *never,* use *rarely, hardly ever, almost never,* or *not usually.*

Example

International students almost never want to go home at the end of a year abroad.

Instead of *always,* use *usually, almost always,* or *often.*

Example

Teenagers are often irresponsible.

Don't use the quantifiers *no, none,* or *all* when you are giving your opinion about something. Instead, use *very few, hardly any, almost no,* or *almost none.*

Example

Very few international students learn English easily.

Instead of *all*, use *almost all, most,* or *many.*

Example

Many international students work harder than other students.

6 Correcting Overgeneralizations Rewrite the following sentences so that they are not overgeneralizations. Use adverbs of frequency and/or quantifiers.

1. All international students have a difficult time their first year.
   Many international students have a difficult time their first year.
2. International students never become friendly with native-speaking students.
   ____
3. All international students get better grades than other students.
   ____
4. Professors never understand students from other countries.
   ____
5. International students always feel isolated.
   ____
6. All students in city colleges are too busy to be friendly.
   ____
7. No four-year colleges offer practical training.
   ____
8. Studying in a foreign language is always very difficult.
   ____
9. All students in community colleges can live at home.
   ____
10. Studying in a private college is always extremely expensive.
   ____

WRITING WITH COMPUTERS

If you need to verify information while you are writing or preparing to write, you can use an online encyclopedia. Open a search engine and enter the word **encyclopedia** to see many different options. Be sure to use a reputable source.

Strategy

Writing the First Draft

Once you have developed and organized your ideas, you are ready to write your paragraph. The first paragraph you write will still need work; we call this paragraph a *draft.* A draft is an intermediate step, not the final product.

7 **Writing the First Draft** Write the first draft of your paragraph on the advantages of large or small colleges. Include reasons for all of your opinions, and use connecting and transition words to join your ideas.

▲ It's easy to find your way around a small college or university campus.

Part 3 Revising and Editing

Revising for Content and Editing for Form

Strategy

Revising for Content

You should review a piece of writing at least twice. The first time, you should revise it for content, and the second time, you should edit it for form. When you revise your writing for content, focus on the ideas. Ask yourself if you have included everything you wanted to write about and if there are any unnecessary details. Also, look at how ideas are connected and organized.

1 **Revising for Content** Look at the paragraph below. Focus only on the content—the writer's ideas and organization. Make comments and suggestions based on the following questions:

1. Does the writer give enough information?
2. Does the topic sentence state the main idea of the paragraph?
3. Does the writer give reasons for his or her opinions?
4. Is the paragraph smooth or choppy?
5. Does the writer use overgeneralizations?

Don't worry about misspelled words and other errors for now.

There are several reasons that undergraduate students should not study away from home living away from home is much more expensive than living at home. Families can save money by not paying room and board, teenagers are not mature enough to live far away from their families. Therefore, they often get into trouble. Some students even fail courses because they are not disciplined enough to study in addition they never go to class. Finally many students feel lonely and homesick So they are not able to study. All undergraduate students who stay home with their families get a good education and also a good price.

Strategy

Editing for Form

When you edit writing for form, focus on how the writing looks on the page as well as the grammar, spelling, and punctuation.

Following are some guidelines for forming paragraphs:

Guidelines for Forming Paragraphs

(For more rules on capitalization and punctuation, see Appendix 2 and Appendix 3.)

1. Indent the first sentence of your paragraphs.
2. Leave a one-inch left and right margin.
3. Begin each sentence with a capital letter.
4. End each sentence with a period (.), a question mark (?), or an exclamation point (!).
5. Make sure that the end punctuation immediately follows the last word of the sentence.
6. Leave one space between sentences.
7. Double-space the paragraph.

2 Editing for Form Edit the paragraph above for form. Use the guidelines listed above.

Evaluating Your Writing

Strategy

Using Rubrics

A rubric is a set of characteristics you can use to evaluate your writing. To use the rubric, give your writing a score (3 = excellent, 2 = adequate, 1 = developing) for each characteristic.

3 Using a Rubric Read the rubric below with your class. Then use the rubric to score your paragraph.

Score	Description
3 **Excellent**	▪ **Content:** Paragraph presents advantages of large or small colleges and clear reasons for opinions. ▪ **Organization:** Paragraph includes a clear topic sentence that states the reader's opinion. All sentences connect to the topic sentence and are organized from most to least important. ▪ **Vocabulary:** Vocabulary is specific, varied, and used correctly throughout. ▪ **Grammar:** Present tense verbs are correct. Transition and connecting words and phrases are used effectively. There are very few grammar problems, and meaning is clear. ▪ **Spelling and Mechanics:** Most words are spelled correctly, and punctuation is correct. Guidelines for correct paragraph form are followed.
2 **Adequate**	▪ **Content:** Paragraph presents advantages of large or small colleges and reasons for most opinions. ▪ **Organization:** Paragraph has a topic sentence, but opinion may not be stated. Some sentences may not connect to main idea. Sentences may not be organized from most to least important. ▪ **Vocabulary:** Vocabulary is clear and specific, but some words might be used incorrectly. ▪ **Grammar:** Most present tense verbs are correct. Transitions and connectors may be used, but there may be some mistakes. ▪ **Spelling and Mechanics:** There are some distracting spelling or punctuation mistakes, and there may be some mistakes in paragraph form.

1 Developing	■ **Content:** Paragraph does not present the advantages of large or small colleges, or reasons for opinions are not included. ■ **Organization:** Paragraph ideas do not connect to the topic sentence, or there is no topic sentence. Order of ideas is unclear. ■ **Vocabulary:** Vocabulary is limited, and there are too many mistakes to understand the ideas. ■ **Grammar:** There are many grammar problems, which makes writing confusing to the reader. Writing is choppy because transition words and connectors are not used. ■ **Spelling and Mechanics:** Many distracting spelling and punctuation mistakes. Guidelines for correct paragraph form are not followed.

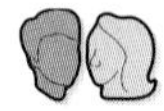

4 Peer Sharing Show your paragraph to another student. Does he or she agree with your opinions? Why? Why not? Do you agree or disagree with your partner's opinions? Why? Why not?

5 Writing the Second Draft Rewrite your paragraph using your rubric evaluation. Then give your paragraph to your teacher for comments and corrections. When your teacher returns your paper, ask him or her about any comments or corrections you don't understand.

Part 4 Expansion Activities

1 Having a Debate Use the paragraphs the class wrote for this chapter for a debate. Follow these steps:

1. Divide into two groups: students who think small colleges are better and students who prefer large colleges.
2. Meet with members of your team, and read each other's paragraphs.
3. Make a list of your team's opinions.
4. Try to guess what the other team will argue, and think of how to counter their arguments. Counterarguments are called *rebuttals*.
5. Choose three students from each team. During the debate, one will give the arguments (about 5 minutes), one will give the rebuttal (about 3 minutes), and one will give a summary of both (about 3 minutes).

2 **Writing About Advantages or Disadvantages** Write a paragraph about the advantages or disadvantages of one of the following topics:

1. small towns / large cities
2. small families / large families
3. owning a car / using public transportation

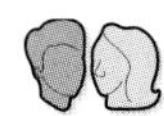

3 **Writing Advertising Copy** Work with a partner to write advertising copy based on a product's advantages. Follow these steps:

1. Look through some magazines and read the advertisements for different products.
2. Choose an ad that describes and shows a product's advantages.
3. Make a list of all the advantages.
4. Give your list and the picture (with the text covered) to a partner. See if he or she can write the text using your list.
5. Then compare your partner's ad with the real ad. How are they different? How are they the same?

Strategy

Journal Writing

Start to keep a journal. In this journal, you will free write. Free writing is when you write whatever ideas come into your head without worrying about grammar or spelling mistakes. Your teacher may ask you to write in your journal in class or at home.

4 **Writing in Your Journal** Choose one of the following topics to write about in your journal for 10 minutes:

1. The advantages and disadvantages of your school.
2. Learning English: What do you like about it? What do you dislike? What do you find difficult? What is easy for you?

5 **Researching Colleges and Universities** You can easily find information about colleges and universities on the Internet. They usually have an address ending in *.edu* (for example, *www.harvard.edu*).

On page 21 is a list of large universities and small colleges. Look up one small college and one large university and compare them. Which one would you rather attend? List your reasons. Share your opinions with your class.

Large Universities	Small Colleges
Ohio State University	Winthrop College
New York University	Hamilton College
University of California at Los Angeles	Evergreen College
University of Colorado	Kenyon College
University of Miami	Pitzer College

Self-Assessment Log

In this chapter, you worked through the activities listed below. How much did they help you to become a better writer? Check *A lot, A little,* or *Not at all.*

	A lot	A little	Not at all
I ranked decision-making factors in order of importance.	❑	❑	❑
I organized ideas in order of importance.	❑	❑	❑
I learned to write a topic sentence for an opinion paragraph.	❑	❑	❑
I practiced using *because, so,* and *therefore* to give reasons.	❑	❑	❑
I listed reasons with *first of all, finally, in addition,* and *also.*	❑	❑	❑
I learned to make general statements.	❑	❑	❑
I learned to avoid overgeneralizations.	❑	❑	❑
I used a writing rubric to evaluate my first draft.	❑	❑	❑
(Add something) ______________________________	❑	❑	❑

____

City Life

In This Chapter

Genre Focus: Descriptive

Writing Product

A descriptive paragraph about where you live

Writing Process

- Use sense details in descriptions.
- Write a topic sentence for a descriptive paragraph.
- Use a mind map to brainstorm and organize ideas.
- Write a concluding sentence for a descriptive paragraph.
- Give reasons with *since*.
- Vary sentence structures within a paragraph.
- Identify and correct comma splices.

"Living together is an art."

—William Pickens
American educator and civil rights advocate (1881–1954)

Connecting to the Topic

1. Is this place similar to where you live? Explain.
2. Does this look like an interesting place to live? Explain.
3. What would be the advantages and disadvantages of living in a place like this?

Part 1 Before You Write

Exploring Ideas

1 Describing Scenes Look at the photos of streets below, and choose one of them to describe. Write as much as you can in 10 minutes. Answer the following questions:

1. What is happening on the street?
2. Would you like to live in this neighborhood? Why or why not?
3. How is the street similar to or different from the street where you live?

▲ A street in Cairo

▲ A street in Berlin

2 Sharing Your Ideas Form a small group with other students who wrote about the same photo you did. Share and discuss what you wrote. Did you notice the same things in the photo? Did you have the same opinion of the scene?

Strategy

Writing About Sense Details and Feelings

In this chapter you are going to write a descriptive paragraph about where you live: your neighborhood, your street, your dormitory, your apartment or house, or your room. A good description includes *sense details*: the things you can see, hear, touch, taste, and smell.

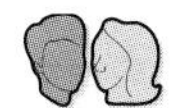

What Do You Think?

Classifying Sense Details

Work with a partner, and test your knowledge of the adjectives below. Put each adjective in the correct category. (Note: Some might fit into more than one category.) Then add some adjectives of your own to each category.

bitter	cramped	noisy	salty	smooth
bright	foul	rotten	soft	spicy
colorful	gloomy	rough	sour	

See	Hear	Smell	Taste	Touch
	noisy			

3 Choosing a Topic Write the name of the place you are going to describe in your descriptive paragraph.

4 Listing Details Make a list of sense details for the place you are going to describe. Use noun phrases and adjectives.

1. What I can see:
   colorful piles of vegetables
   ____
2. What I can hear:
   ____
   ____
3. What I can touch:
   ____
   ____
4. What I can taste (optional):
   ____
   ____
5. What I can smell (optional):
   ____
   ____

5 Describing Feelings In your descriptive paragraph, you will include the feelings and opinions you have about the place you describe. Write a few notes about how you feel about the place you describe. Also write about why you feel the way you do.

Example *My bedroom makes me feel relaxed and calm.*

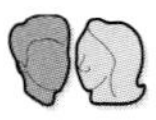

6 Sharing Your Ideas Describe the place you chose to a partner. Help each other get ideas by asking each other questions about the places you described. Add any new ideas you have to your notes.

Building Vocabulary

7 Identifying Descriptive Words and Phrases Read the following paragraph. Notice the effect the details have on the writing. Underline the descriptive words and phrases.

My Neighborhood

My neighborhood is <u>fascinating</u> because people from all over the world live in it. When I walk down the main street of my neighborhood, I can hear the unfamiliar sounds of languages from all over the world. Each ethnic group has its own colorful shop or fascinating restaurant. On a warm evening, I can smell the sweet melons from the Korean produce store and the spicy curries from the Indian restaurant. These smells are free, but for a small price, I can also buy any of 50 kinds of cheeses with strange names from one store, or exotic Asian vegetables and the spices to cook them in from another. The people of the neighborhood take pride in their surroundings. On almost every street, they plant trees and flowers from their native countries to remind them of home and to brighten up the dull gray cement and run-down apartment buildings. One of my neighbors plants delicate Scottish flowers every year in memory of her mother's garden in Scotland. Another neighbor has a Chinese vegetable garden in window boxes. I don't need to buy an airplane ticket to experience the world; a walk around my neighborhood can be just as exciting.

8 Matching Words to Their Definitions Find words or phrases in the paragraph above that mean the following:

1. strange and unusual *exotic*
2. small and pretty ______________
3. very interesting ______________
4. to make pretty ______________

5. sad-looking ______________________

6. to be proud of ______________________

9 **Using Sense Details** Work in groups of three. Choose one of the photos below. Make lists of sense details that describe the neighborhood. Then use those words to describe the photo.

▲ Hong Kong's neighborhoods are lively.

▲ Some villages in Europe don't change much over time.

1. What you can see:

____

____

2. What you can hear:

____

____

3. What you can smell:

____

____

4. What you can taste:

____

____

5. What you can feel:

____

____

Organizing Ideas

Strategy

Writing Topic Sentences

The topic sentence tells the reader the subject of the paragraph. In a descriptive paragraph, the topic sentence is general enough to unite all the descriptive details in the paragraph but focused enough to grab the reader's attention. It should also indicate the writer's feeling about the place.

Instead of using vague, overused adjectives such as *nice, good,* and *bad* in your topic sentences, use more specific and vivid adjectives.

Vague and uninteresting: My neighborhood is a nice place to live.
Specific and interesting: My neighborhood is fascinating because people from many countries live in it.

10 Choosing the Best Topic Sentence For each set of topic sentences below, put a check mark (✔) next to the best topic sentence, the one that is focused and interesting.

1. Topic: "My Room"
   - **a.** _____ My room is a perfect place for one person to live.
   - **b.** _____ Many people live in single rooms.
   - **c.** _____ My room is nice.
   - **d.** _____ I love the big windows.
2. Topic: "My House"
   - **a.** _____ There are a lot of houses like mine in my neighborhood.
   - **b.** _____ I love my house because it is filled with happy memories.
   - **c.** _____ Big houses are best.
   - **d.** _____ My family lives in a good house.
3. Topic: "My Dormitory"
   - **a.** _____ My dormitory has never felt like home to me.
   - **b.** _____ I live in a dormitory.
   - **c.** _____ Dormitories are where students live.
   - **d.** _____ The cafeteria food in my dormitory is good.

11 **Writing and Sharing a Draft Topic Sentence** Write a draft topic sentence for your own descriptive paragraph. Then in small groups, discuss each other's topic sentences. Answer the following questions:

1. Does the topic sentence introduce the place to be described?
2. Does it grab the reader's attention?
3. Does it indicate the writer's feeling about the place?

Using Graphic Organizers

Strategy

Using a Graphic Organizer to Organize Details for a Paragraph
One way to brainstorm and organize ideas for a focused descriptive paragraph is to use a graphic organizer. Graphic organizers show how ideas are connected to each other.

The graphic organizer below is called a *mind map.* In the mind map, the topic sentence is in the center. The main supporting details are connected directly to the topic sentence. The secondary details are connected to the main details.

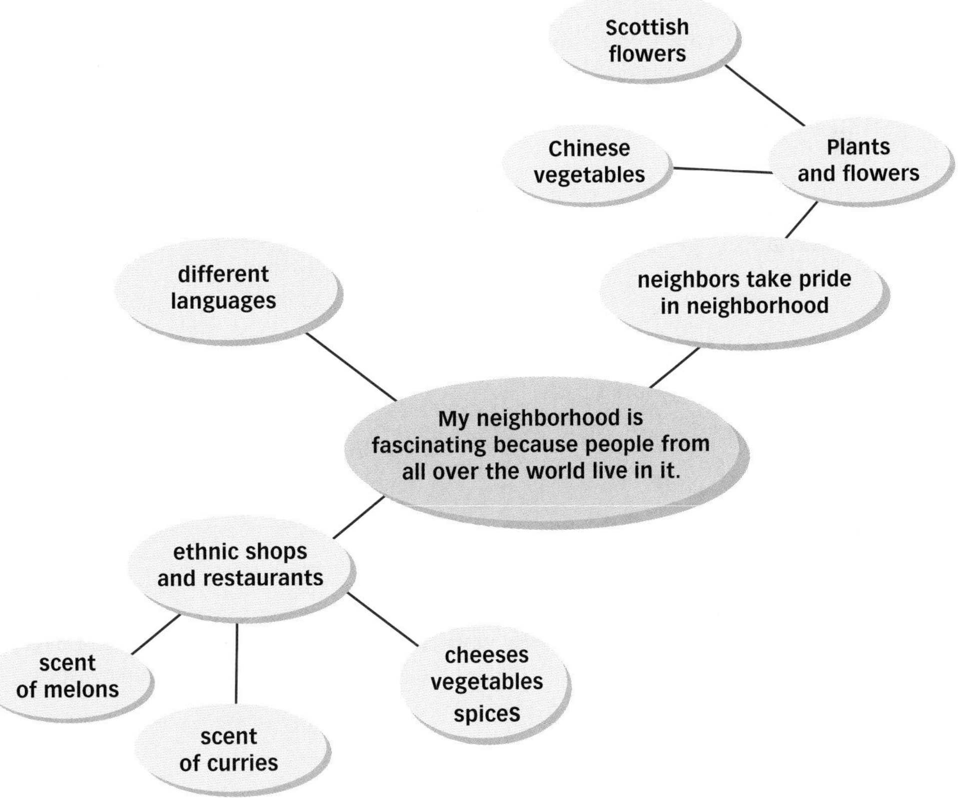

12 Creating a Graphic Organizer On a separate piece of paper, create a mind map for your descriptive paragraph. Write your topic sentence in the middle circle, and connect the main details and secondary details using circles and lines.

Strategy

Getting Rid of Irrelevant Details

All the details in a paragraph should develop the idea stated in the topic sentence. You can use your mind map to identify information that is irrelevant. Look for ideas that are not connected to anything else or only have a loose connection to a main idea, and cross them out.

13 Identifying Irrelevant and Missing Information Some of the information in the graphic organizer below is not related to the topic. Cross it out. Where could the writer add more details?

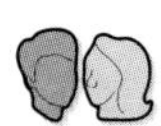

14 Sharing Your Graphic Organizer Show your mind map to a partner. Does your partner think that all the ideas are related to the topic? Does he or she think you need any more details?

Strategy

Writing Concluding Sentences

Most paragraphs have concluding sentences that repeat the idea of the topic sentence in different words. Below is the concluding sentence from the paragraph on page 26 about a neighborhood. Note that it repeats the idea of the topic sentence in different words. In that way, it summarizes the main point of the paragraph.

Example

> I don't need to buy an airplane ticket to experience the world; a walk around my neighborhood can be just as exciting.

Other concluding sentences give a personal reaction to the topic of the paragraph. Below is a concluding sentence for a paragraph about a Brazilian student's experience living in a dormitory at an Australian college. Note that it includes a personal opinion.

Example

> Even though it was sometimes too noisy and crowded, I enjoyed living in my dormitory because of all of the friends I made.

15 **Writing Concluding Sentences** Read the paragraph below. Then write three possible concluding sentences. Share your ideas with a group of three.

Muscat, the ancient capital of Oman, is on a spectacular site. The city lies on a narrow strip of land between the sparkling blue waters of the Arabian Gulf and the rocky brown mountains behind it. Muscat is a wonderful combination of historic sites and modern buildings. Tourists interested in history will marvel at the splendid forts with their watchtowers and walled gateways. Those with an interest in contemporary architecture will appreciate the simple lines of the Sultan's lovely but unpretentious palace. Directly adjacent to Muscat is the harbor of Muttrah with its beautiful corniche and busy market full of the sights and sounds of this ancient bridge between the Middle East and Asia.

▲ The corniche in Muttrah Souq, Oman

Part 2 Developing Writing Skills

Developing Cohesion and Clarity

GIVING REASONS WITH *SINCE*

Because and *since* have almost the same meaning when *since* doesn't refer to a point of time in the past. They both express a cause.

Because and *since* often introduce a dependent clause in complex sentences. Dependent clauses are clauses that contain a subject and a verb but cannot stand alone.

Look at the following examples of complex sentences with *since*. The dependent clauses are underlined.

Examples

Since quite a few people in the neighborhood come from the Middle East, there are many great Middle Eastern shops and restaurants here.

There are many great Middle Eastern shops and restaurants here *since* quite a few people in the neighborhood come from the Middle East.

Note that a dependent clause with *since* can come at the beginning or end of a sentence. If it comes at the beginning of a sentence, it is followed by a comma. A comma isn't needed if the clause comes at the end of the sentence.

1 Combining Sentences Using *Since* Combine the sentences below using *since*. More than one answer is correct.

1. Many people have lived in my neighborhood for years. It is a very friendly place.
   Since many people have lived in my neighborhood for years, it is a very friendly place.
2. My apartment is small. I have to keep it very neat.
   ____
   ____
3. My cousin needed a roommate and is easy to get along with. I decided to move in with him.
   ____
   ____
4. It is easy to get to know everyone in my dormitory. Only 40 people live in it.
   ____
   ____

5. I have many relatives in the city. I decided not to live in a dormitory.

____

____

Strategy

Varying Sentence Structure

If most of the sentences in a paragraph are structured the same way or repeat the same words, the paragraph may be boring to read.

Example

My neighborhood is a wonderful place to eat and shop for food because people from all over the world live there. It is interesting because it has many ethnic restaurants because people come from many countries. It is also the best place to go when you want some good Chinese, Italian, Middle Eastern Vietnamese, or Polish food. My neighborhood is the greatest when you want to buy many kinds of international foods. You can buy delicious cheeses and sausages at the Italian store on the corner of my block. You can buy sweet melons and all kinds of fresh vegetables from the Korean produce store two blocks from my apartment. You can also buy delicious kebabs and baklava from the Lebanese restaurant across the street. Why would I want to live anywhere else when everything I need is right in my neighborhood?

In this paragraph, words are repeated, and the same sentence structure (subject-verb) is used throughout. This makes the paragraph repetitive and uninteresting. You can make the paragraph more interesting by varying the sentence structure. For example, you can begin some of the sentences with dependent clauses beginning with words like *because, since,* and *when* or prepositional phrases beginning with words such as *at, in, on, from,* or *with.*

2 Varying Sentence Structure Rewrite the following sentences. Change the sentence structure by moving the dependent clause or prepositional phrase to the beginning of each sentence.

1. I always see interesting people when I take a walk in my neighborhood.

   When I take a walk in my neighborhood, I always see interesting people.

   ____

2. I never liked Chinese food before I moved to this neighborhood.

   ____

   ____

3. I have become used to the sounds of traffic since I moved to the city.

____

____

4. You can find newspapers from all over the world on any street corner.

____

____

5. My neighborhood is quite diverse because almost all of my neighbors are from a different country.

____

____

3 **Identifying Dependent Clauses** Look at the paragraph in Activity 7 on page 26. Underline the sentences that begin with dependent clauses or prepositional phrases. Look for words such as *because, since, when, at, in, on, from,* and *with.*

WRITING WITH COMPUTERS

When you write the first draft of your paragraph on a computer, set the line spacing to double space so that you will have room to make notes and corrections.

4 **Varying Sentence Structure in a Paragraph** Rewrite the example paragraph on page 33. Use dependent clauses to vary the sentence structure in some of the sentences. Then compare your paragraph with a classmate's. Did you change the paragraph in the same way?

5 **Writing the First Draft** Write your paragraph using the topic sentence you wrote and the information from your graphic organizer. Make your paragraph interesting by using vivid sensory details and varying sentence structure.

Part 3 Revising and Editing

Strategy

Revising with the Topic Sentence in Mind

All of the sentences in a paragraph should develop the main idea in the topic sentence. If they don't, there are two things you can do:

1. If you find that you started to write about an idea that is different from the idea in your topic sentence, and you like the new idea, you can change your topic sentence to reflect the new idea.
2. If some of your sentences are not about the idea in your topic sentence, change or delete those sentences.

Revising for Content and Editing for Form

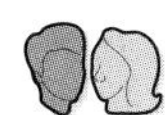

1 Revising for Content Revise the following paragraph for content. Decide whether some sentences need to be removed or whether the topic sentence should be changed. Cross out sentences that don't belong or rewrite the topic sentence. Discuss your changes with a partner.

▲ A suburban community in the United States

We live in an ordinary house on an ordinary street in an ordinary suburb, and I think it is terrific! Our house is now about 30 years old, but it looks newer. I used to live in apartments, first in Florida, and then in New Mexico. But I prefer living in our own home. My house is like hundreds of other houses in the suburbs, one story with an attached garage. There is nothing special about the house, and it won't win any prizes for architecture, but it's perfect for our family. The kitchen is big and has new appliances, including a beautiful new dishwasher and a microwave oven. I don't like the heat, but we have air conditioning in the living room and bedrooms, so it is always cool. I don't know why some people I know don't like the suburbs. For the kids, there's a nice yard where they can play. It's very safe, so my wife and I don't have to worry. I am very thankful that we can afford this house and live our ordinary lives in it.

CORRECTING COMMA SPLICES

A comma splice is an incorrect sentence made of two independent clauses connected with a comma. An independent clause has a subject and a verb and can stand alone.

Comma splice: I am living in a dormitory room, it is much too small for my roommate and me.
Comma splice: First you notice all the exciting sights, later you notice the dirt.

You can correct a comma splice in at least three ways:

1. Change the comma to a period or a semicolon.

Examples

I am living in a dormitory room. It is much too small for my roommate and me.
First you notice all the exciting sights; later you notice the dirt.

2. Change the comma splice into a sentence with a dependent clause. The dependent clause is underlined in the example.

Example

I am living in a dormitory room that is much too small for my roommate and me.

In the example above, the dependent clause describes the noun *dormitory room.* The pronoun *that* replaces it.

3. Use a conjunction such as *and*, *but*, or *so* to connect the two independent clauses.

Note that a comma usually comes before the conjunction.

Example

First you notice all the exciting sights, and later you notice the dirt.

The following words cannot be used to join two independent clauses. Check for them when you edit:

then however therefore later

---

2 Correcting Comma Splices Correct the comma splices below using one of the three methods listed in the previous section.

1. My suburban apartment is big and sunny; it has a living room with large windows filled with plants.
2. I have a roommate who is very sloppy, she never washes the dishes, and she leaves her clothes all over the apartment.
3. I like my street because my neighbors are wonderful, they will help anybody who is having problems.
4. First I painted my room a pale blue, later I made new curtains.
5. My favorite place to relax is the park, it is up the hill from my apartment.
6. My street is dirty and noisy, however it has many good restaurants and my neighbors are friendly.

3 Editing for Form Edit the paragraph below for form. Rewrite the paragraph fixing the sentences that have comma splices.

My neighborhood is a fascinating place, it is in one of the biggest cities in the world, New York City, however, there is a small-town feeling to it. Most of the buildings in the neighborhood are small brick apartment houses, they have peeling red and brown paint. Many of the people here have lived in the neighborhood for years, they know each other and take pride in the neighborhood. They have planted trees and flowers in front of the buildings, they have built benches where the old people sit and talk. Since many of the people are from Germany and Eastern Europe, there are wonderful German, Hungarian, and Polish shops here. I wouldn't want to live in any other neighborhood of the city.

Evaluating Your Writing

4 Using a Rubric Read the rubric below with your class. Then use the rubric to score your paragraph.

Score	Description
3 **Excellent**	■ **Content:** Paragraph vividly describes where writer lives and the writer's feeling about the place. ■ **Organization:** A topic sentence introduces the main idea of paragraph, and all details develop this main idea. Related details are grouped together. There is a concluding sentence. ■ **Vocabulary:** Description includes vivid sensory details. Words are used correctly throughout. ■ **Grammar:** Sentence structure is varied, and there are no comma splices. ■ **Spelling and Mechanics:** Most words are spelled correctly, and punctuation is correct throughout.
2 **Adequate**	■ **Content:** Paragraph describes where writer lives but may not express writer's feeling about the place. May be lacking some detail. ■ **Organization:** Paragraph ideas are introduced by a topic sentence, but the topic sentence may be vague or uninteresting. Related ideas are mostly grouped together. Paragraph has a concluding sentence, but it may be weak. ■ **Vocabulary:** Description includes some vivid details, but some words may be used incorrectly. ■ **Grammar:** Sentence structure is somewhat varied. Paragraph may have one comma splice. ■ **Spelling and Mechanics:** Paragraph includes some spelling or punctuation mistakes.
1 **Developing**	■ **Content:** Paragraph does not describe where writer lives or does not express writer's feeling about the place. ■ **Organization:** Paragraph doesn't include a topic sentence, or paragraph ideas do not connect to the topic sentence. Ideas are not in coherent order. There is no concluding sentence. ■ **Vocabulary:** Description does not include vivid sensory details. Many words are used incorrectly, making the paragraph difficult to understand. ■ **Grammar:** Sentence structure is not varied. Paragraph includes comma splices or other grammatical errors, making the paragraph difficult to understand. ■ **Spelling and Mechanics:** Paragraph includes many distracting spelling and punctuation mistakes.

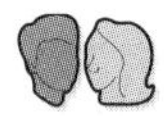

5 Peer Sharing Share your paragraph with another student. Discuss the following questions:

1. Do you understand why the writer feels the way he or she does about the place described?
2. Would you like to visit this place? Why or why not?
3. What else would you like to know about the place?

6 Writing the Second Draft Rewrite your paragraph using your rubric evaluation. Then give your paragraph to your teacher for comments and corrections. When your teacher returns your paper, ask him or her about any comments or corrections you don't understand.

TOEFL® IBT

Focus on Testing

Brainstorming for Ideas

In this chapter, you practiced writing topic sentences and adding details to a paragraph. When you're taking a test, you have little time to do these things. So take some time before you write to brainstorm. First, list all the ideas that come to your mind about the topic. Then read your list, and see what main idea it suggests. Cross out any ideas that don't fit. Use your main idea to write a topic sentence. Use the rest of your ideas to develop your paragraph; group the ones that go together, and number them in the order you want to write about them.

Practice Choose a topic from the list below. Then spend the first 4 minutes brainstorming ideas for the topic. First, write all of your ideas down. Then go back and decide on a main idea. Next write a topic sentence.

Topics

A description of your school

A description of your favorite place

Part 4 Expansion Activities

1 Writing New Paragraph Openers and Closers Look at the paragraphs in a description of a place in a travel brochure. Find the topic sentence and concluding sentence of one paragraph. Write a new topic sentence and a new concluding sentence for the paragraph.

2 Analyzing Descriptions Find descriptions of people, places, or things. Which descriptions are personal (including feelings and opinions)? Which descriptions are impersonal (including facts, not feelings)? Did the writer use sense details? If so, how?

3 Guessing the Object Write a brief description of a common object: for example, a pencil, a brick wall, or a telephone. Don't write the name of the object, but include as many details as possible in the description. In small groups, take turns reading your descriptions. Can your classmates guess what you are describing?

4 Writing in Your Journal Write in your journal about one or both of the following topics:

1. Write two descriptions of a person you know. Write each description in 10 minutes. Make the first impersonal, including only facts. Make the second personal, including feelings and opinions.
2. Think of one of your earliest childhood memories. Make notes, and then write a paragraph describing your memory in as much detail as possible.

▲ An early childhood memory

5 **Researching Neighborhoods** Work in groups. Use a search engine to find information on the Internet about the neighborhoods in a large city. Use the words *neighborhood* + (the name of the city) + *map* + *tourist* to search. Each person in the group should write a paragraph about one of the following:

1. An ethnic neighborhood
2. An historic neighborhood
3. A neighborhood with many restaurants
4. A good neighborhood for shopping
5. A neighborhood with many artists and/or young people

▲ A neighborhood in New Orleans

Self-Assessment Log

In this chapter, you worked through the activities listed below. How much did they help you to become a better writer? Check *A lot, A little,* or *Not at all.*

	A lot	**A little**	**Not at all**
I learned to use sense details in descriptions.	❑	❑	❑
I learned about topic sentences for descriptive paragraphs.	❑	❑	❑
I used a mind map to brainstorm and organize ideas.	❑	❑	❑
I learned to write a concluding sentence.	❑	❑	❑
I learned to give reasons with *since.*	❑	❑	❑
I learned how to vary sentence structures within a paragraph.	❑	❑	❑
I learned how to identify and correct comma splices.	❑	❑	❑
I used a writing rubric to evaluate my first draft.	❑	❑	❑
(Add something) ______________________________	❑	❑	❑

____

Business and Money

In This Chapter

Genre Focus: Argument

Writing Product

A letter in response to a web page article

Writing Process

- Practice free writing.
- Read and discuss a web page article.
- Use a graphic organizer to connect opinions and reasons.
- Express obligations and give advice with *must, have to,* and *should.*
- Support an opinion with examples and predictions.
- Identify and avoid faulty reasoning.
- Identify and correct hyphenation errors.

"Money speaks sense in a language all nations understand."

—Aphra Behn
English novelist and dramatist (1640–1689)

Connecting to the Topic

1. Do you think money is equally important to people all over the world? Why or why not?
2. How important is money to you?
3. How does money impact your life?

Part 1 Before You Write

Exploring Ideas

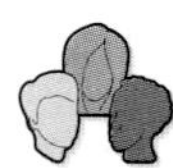

1 Discussing Attitudes Toward Money In small groups, read and discuss the quotations below by famous thinkers. Do you agree with them or not? What attitude toward money does each one express?

1. "Time is money."
   —Benjamin Franklin
   American diplomat and philosopher (1706–1790)
2. "Money speaks sense in a language all nations understand."
   —Aphra Behn
   English writer (1640–1689)
3. "Capital as such is not evil; it is its wrong use that is evil. Capital in some form or other will always be needed."
   —Mohandas Gandhi
   Indian nationalist leader (1869–1948)
4. "It has been said that the love of money is the root of all evil."
   —Samuel Butler
   English novelist (1835–1902)
5. "Money buys everything except love, personality, freedom, immortality, silence, peace."
   —Carl Sandburg
   American poet and biographer (1878–1967)

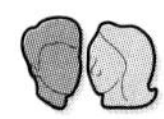

2 Discussing a Quotation Think of another quotation or proverb about money. Discuss it with a partner. What attitudes toward money does it show?

Strategy

Free Writing

Free writing is a good way to generate ideas on a topic before you write. When you free write, you write as fast as you can without thinking too much about what you're writing or where you're headed. You do not need to think about grammar and vocabulary. You also do not have to worry about connecting your ideas. You can sometimes come up with your best ideas when you allow yourself to free write.

3 Free Writing Free write for 10 minutes about your own attitudes toward money.

4 Discussing a Web Page Article In this chapter, you are going to write a letter to the editor of a web page about your reaction to the article on page 45. In small groups, read the article and take turns discussing each person's reaction to the event it describes.

October 29, 20___

Luck or Thievery?

COLUMBUS, OHIO. October 28 was a lucky day for motorists driving along Interstate 71 at about 9:30 in the morning. As a truck from the Metropolitan Armored Car Company sped down the highway, its back door blew open, and bags of money fell onto the road. When other vehicles hit the bags, the bags split open, spewing over a million dollars all over the highway.

▲ An armored truck spilled bags of money on Interstate 71.

It didn't take motorists long to realize that the paper swirling around them was cash. They stopped on and around the highway and scooped up handfuls of money, gleefully putting $20, $50, $100, even $1,000 dollar bills into bags, pockets, and purses. When the police arrived, they estimated that over two hundred people had been helping themselves to the bonanza.

Officials hoping to recover the money were not so gleeful. Columbus Mayor Dana G. Rinehart called the motorists who took the money thieves and said, "May they have many sleepless nights." He states the government will prosecute anyone the police can find.

To encourage the return of the money, Metropolitan Armored Car Company has offered a reward of 10% of all the money they receive. So far, however, they have received only $100,000 from about thirty different people. One man gave back $57,000. Another man, however, called to say he was set for life and was leaving town. Since the cash was insured and belonged to local banks, many people can't see that they are hurting anyone by keeping it.

Even if the government prosecutes, it will have trouble convicting the thieves. "Probably two-thirds of the jurors would think the defendants should have kept the money," said prosecutor Michael Miller.

Building Vocabulary

5 Matching Words to Their Definitions In the web page article on page 45, underline the words listed below. Use the context to help you guess the meaning. Then match the words with their meanings.

1. __h__	armored	a. very happy
2. _____	split	b. pick up
3. _____	spew	c. charge with a crime
4. _____	recover	d. tear open
5. _____	scoop up	e. find
6. _____	gleeful	f. spill
7. _____	bonanza	g. sudden riches
8. _____	prosecute	h. protected with strong metal
9. _____	convict	i. find guilty of a crime
10. _____	insured	j. protected from loss

6 Using a Vocabulary Chart In your letter to the editor, you might want to use some of the words above. First put each of them in the correct column below. Then write sentences with five of the words, giving your opinion of the happenings in the article.

Noun	Verbs	Adjectives
_____	_____	*insured*
	_____	_____
	_____	_____
	_____	
	_____	
	_____	

Example

Even though the money was insured, the drivers shouldn't have taken it.

____

____

____

____

Organizing Ideas

7 Writing Your Opinion and Reasons Do you think the motorists should return the money? On the lines below, write reasons why or why not.

▲ Motorists help themselves to the bonanza.

____

____

____

____

8 Discussing the Topic Discuss the following questions in small groups:

1. Is it wrong to keep money that you haven't earned?
2. What does it mean that the money is insured? Who will pay the money back?
3. Is it true that the loss of the money doesn't hurt anyone?
4. What would you have done if you were one of the motorists? Would you have taken the money? What would you do if you were an official of the town?

Using Graphic Organizers

9 **Using a Graphic Organizer** Summarize your group's discussion in Activity 8 by writing the ideas into the graphic organizer below. If you have any more ideas, add them.

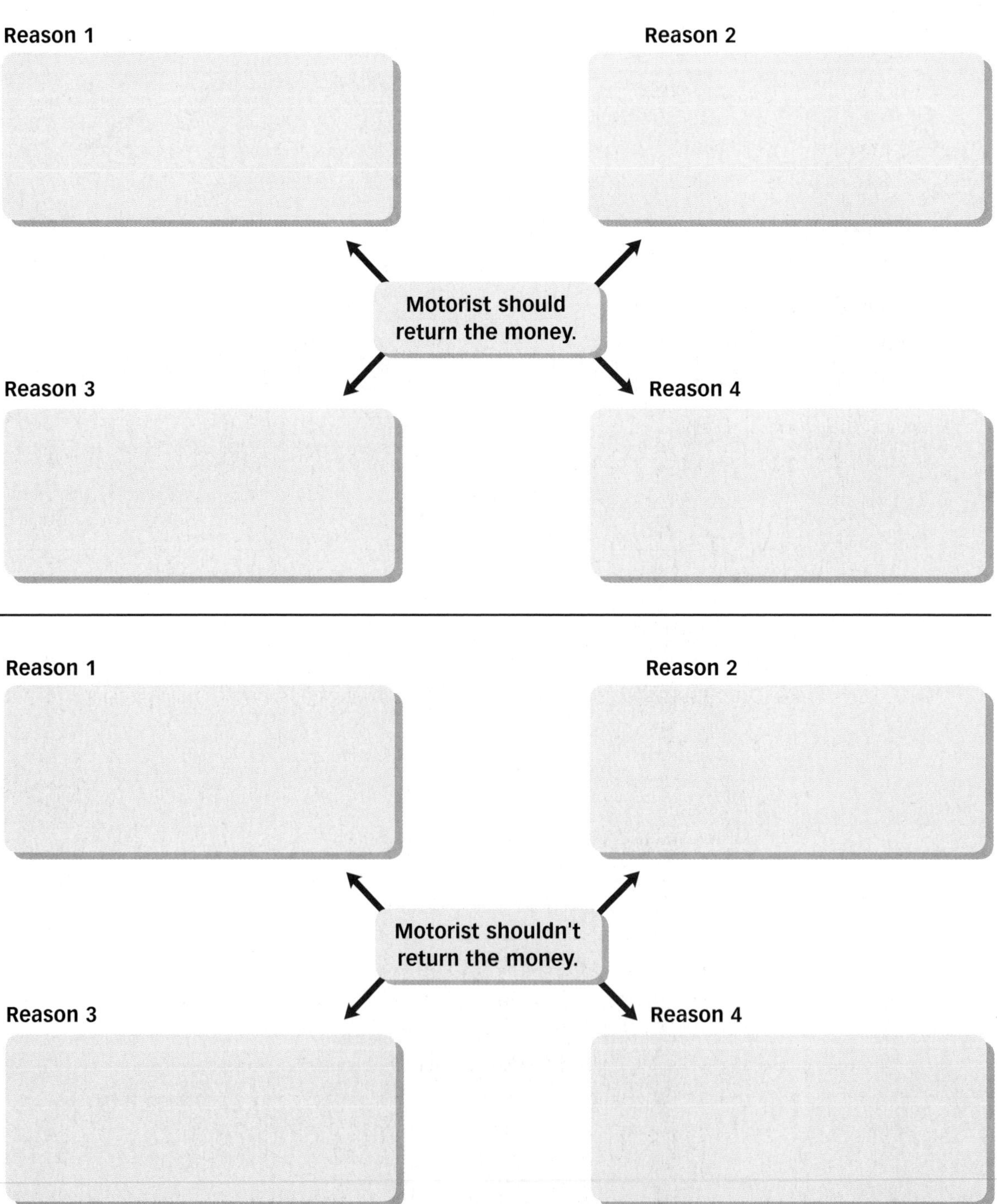

10 **Analyzing the Organization of a Letter to the Editor** Read the letter below written to the editor of a newspaper. Then answer the questions that follow.

October 30, 20___

Dear Editor,

Regarding the article about people who don't pay taxes on money they make from small home businesses (*Government Targets Small Business Owners*, Oct. 23), my opinion is that the government should stay out of at least one part of our lives—our income!

First of all, most people who run small businesses are honest, law-abiding citizens. Many of them have other jobs where they pay more than their share of taxes (unlike the very wealthy, who find ways to pay almost no taxes). Others are people who want jobs where taxes are automatically taken out of their paychecks but can't find them.

Secondly, the government requires too much paperwork from small businesses. If these businesspeople have to keep the complicated records that the tax people require, they won't have time to sell old furniture, prepare food for parties, or whatever their business involves.

Finally, and most importantly, this is supposed to be a free country, but the government interferes everywhere. Let us be free at least in our own homes!

Sincerely,
Al Melinowski
Miami

▲ Diana Baker owns a small business that prepares tax returns.

1. How does the letter begin? What specific information does the author provide to make sure the editor knows what his letter is about?
2. How many paragraphs does the letter have? Note that paragraphs in newspapers are often shorter than paragraphs in academic writing.
3. What does each paragraph contain?
4. What transitional phrases does the writer use to introduce each paragraph? What effect does this have on the flow of the letter?
5. How does the writer support his opinions?

11 Writing an Opening Sentence Write an opening sentence for your letter responding to the article, "Luck or Thievery?" Begin with a phrase telling which article you are responding to. Use the letter in Activity 10 as a model.

____

____

12 Giving Reasons for Your Opinion Now give two or three reasons for your opinion. Use the information in your graphic organizer to help you.

____

____

____

____

____

____

Part 2 Developing Writing Skills

Developing Cohesion and Clarity

EXPRESSING OBLIGATION AND GIVING ADVICE WITH MODALS: *MUST, HAVE TO,* AND *SHOULD*

Giving Advice

You can give advice using the modals *should* and *shouldn't.*

Examples

You should do your homework every night.

You shouldn't spend a lot of money. You need to save it for a vacation.

Expressing Obligation

You can express obligation using the modals *have to, don't have to,* and *must.* Expressing obligation means stating whether an action is necessary or not necessary.

Examples

We have to turn in our papers tomorrow. We don't have to type them.

They must arrive on time, or we will leave without them.

1 Evaluating Modals Find an example of *should* and an example of *have to* in the letter to the editor on page 49. Why do you think the writer used those modals in each situation?

2 Using Modals in Sentences

Write a sentence using *must, must not, have to, not have to, should,* or *should not* about the following topics:

1. paying taxes

   Everyone should pay taxes no matter how much money he or she makes.

2. drinking alcohol and then driving

   ____

3. spending a lot of money to clean up the environment

   ____

4. giving money to the poor

   ____

5. lying

   ____

6. trying to find the owner of jewelry found on the street

   ____

7. robbing a person's house if you need money

   ____

8. borrowing someone's car

   ____

Strategy

Supporting an Opinion with Examples

A general truth is a statement of opinion that a lot of people would agree with. When you write general truths, since they are still opinions, not facts, you should follow them with a supporting example.

Example

Most people would like to have more money. That is why lotteries are so popular.

general truth — *supporting example*

3 Identifying General Truths and Examples Look at the second paragraph in the letter to the editor in Activity 10 on page 49. It states a general truth and then supports it with examples. What is the general truth? What are the examples?

General Truth

____

____

Examples

____

____

____

4 Writing Examples The following statements are opinions that could be considered general truths. Give one example to support each of them.

1. The government loses millions of dollars every year because of people who don't pay their share of taxes.

   Many people who work independently don't pay enough taxes.

   ____

2. Almost everyone lies in one way or another.

   ____

   ____

3. Money is the root of all evil.

   ____

   ____

4. Lack of money is the cause of many problems in our society.

   ____

   ____

5. If you find something, it's yours.

   ____

   ____

5 Supporting Your Opinions with Examples Look at the reasons you gave in Activity 7 on page 47 for your opinion on the newspaper article. Can you support any of them with examples? Write them down.

____

____

____

6 **Supporting an Opinion with Predictions** Look at the third paragraph in the letter to the editor in Activity 10 on page 49. It supports an opinion with a prediction. Answer the questions below.

1. What is the prediction?

____

2. What verb tense is used in the *if*–clause?

____

3. What verb tense is used in the main clause?

____

7 **Making Predictions** In small groups, make predictions. What will happen if . . .

1. the government makes the wealthy pay more taxes?
2. the government gives poor people less money?
3. everyone gives one-tenth of his or her income to charity?
4. there are fewer drunk drivers on the road?
5. the government makes smoking completely illegal?

8 **Using Predictions to Support Your Opinion** Look at the reasons you gave for your opinion on the web page article. Can you add to them with predictions? Write two predictions to support your opinions.

TOEFL® IBT

Focus on Testing

Stating a Point of View (even if you don't have one)

In this chapter, you learned ways to state opinions. Good statements of opinion can improve your score for the independent writing task on the TOEFL® Internet-Based Test (iBT).

Read the following sample prompt:

> *In your opinion, what is the most cost-effective way to travel on a university campus—on foot, by bicycle, by car, or by bus? In other words, what method combines reasonable costs (of money, time, and effort) with enough benefits? Support your point of view with specific reasons and examples.*

This prompt, like many others, assumes you have an opinion on the topic. But what if you don't have an opinion about the costs of getting around on campus? Or what if you think that you can't choose unless you know other factors, such as the size and location of the campus?

Below are some strategies for successfully responding to a prompt when you (1) don't have an opinion or (2) think the best answer depends on factors that don't appear in the prompt:

1. **Make up an opinion.** Don't tell your readers that you don't have one. Confidently pretend to have an opinion. You are being tested on your writing abilities, not on whether you have an opinion.
2. **Choose an opinion you can support.** Do not choose a difficult or unfamiliar topic to write about. For example, if you do not know how bus systems on campuses work, do not write about it. Write about what you know or what you can easily imagine.
3. **Write about one point of view, not two.** The prompt asks you to state a preference, not compare or balance two possibilities. A statement like, "In some ways, traveling by foot is more economical on campus, but in other ways traveling by bike is better . . . " leads to a weak response. It does not make a single, strong point. A response with this main idea statement would probably get a low score for being off topic.

Practice After reading each prompt below, set a timer for 5 minutes. During that time, choose a point of view for that task, and write a strong, clear main idea statement related to the prompt.

1. Most U.S. colleges and universities require electives. These are courses outside a student's major field of study. Electives are meant to broaden students' knowledge. However, some students complain that electives cost a lot of money and are unnecessary. In your opinion, are electives good or bad? Why?
2. Some college students pay for newspapers or a cable television service to get current news reports. Others use cost-free Internet sources to get their news. Which source of news do you think is best? Support your opinion with specific reasons and examples.
3. Many college campuses allow businesses to participate in "job fairs." At job fairs, students can meet company representatives and explore job possibilities. Some students and professors object to job fairs because they focus on money, not on learning. What is your opinion? Support your response with specific examples and reasons.

Strategy

Stating Opinions: Strong and Moderate

Some letters to the editor express opinions strongly and others do so moderately. A strong opinion does not usually allow for different points of view, whereas a moderate opinion does. When writers express their opinions strongly, they often use more emotional arguments and may sometimes exaggerate. When writers express their opinions moderately, they use more logical arguments that are often more effective.

9 Evaluating Expressions Read the following expressions. Which of them could be used with strong opinions? Which could be used to express more moderate opinions? How can you tell?

	Strong	Moderate
1. I disagree with ______________.	❑	☑
2. ______________ is total nonsense.	❑	❑
3. My opinion is that ______________.	❑	❑
4. ______________ is immoral.	❑	❑
5. ______________ is the most logical solution.	❑	❑
6. Only a fool would disagree with ______________.	❑	❑
7. I believe ______________.	❑	❑
8. In my opinion ______________.	❑	❑
9. ______________ is completely absurd.	❑	❑

10 Using Expressions of Opinion Write three sentences about the web page article "Luck or Thievery?" using the expressions in Activity 9. Which do you think are more appropriate for your letter?

1. *In my opinion, the people who took the money should return it immediately.*
2. ______________________________
3. ______________________________
4. ______________________________

11 Writing the First Draft Write your letter in response to the web page article on page 45. Use the opening sentence you wrote in Activity 11 on page 50. Give your opinions along with the reasons and examples to support them.

Part 3 Revising and Editing

Revising for Content and Editing for Form

Strategy

Avoiding Faulty Reasoning

When you revise a piece of writing that includes reasons that support opinions, you should make sure that you haven't used faulty reasoning. Following are definitions and examples of different kinds of faulty reasoning.

1. False analogy: assuming that two things are similar in all ways just because they are similar in one or two ways.

Example

Opinion: Dancing is the same as fighting.
Reason: Both are done with a partner.

This is a false analogy. Just because both activities include two people does not mean they are the same.

2. Overgeneralization: saying that something is true for all people or situations when it is only true for some, or making a general statement based on only a few cases.

Example

Opinion: Rich men aren't generous.
Reason: There is a wealthy man who comes into the restaurant where I am a waiter, and he never leaves a tip.

This is an overgeneralization. The opinion is based on the case of only one person.

3. Irrelevant argument: giving an example or reason that does not relate to the opinion.

Example

Opinion: I don't think the accountant was the one who stole money from the company.
Reason: She is so nice. She always says *hello* to me.

The fact that a person is friendly and seems nice has nothing to do with whether she is capable of stealing.

An irrelevant argument might also suggest that, because one event follows another, it relates to it, when it really doesn't.

Example

Opinion: Borrowing money always causes problems.

Reason: Two days after Mario borrowed money from a friend, he had a car accident.

Obviously, Mario's car accident was not caused by borrowing money.

4. Circular reasoning: giving a reason that only restates the opinion in different words.

Example

Opinion: Peter never lies.

Reason: He is always truthful.

In the example above, the reason is a restatement of the opinion. This is circular reasoning.

1 Identifying Faulty Reasoning The following statements are responses to the web page article, "Luck or Thievery?" Identify the kind of faulty reasoning each one shows.

1. Everyone should return the money because the money should go back to the bank.

   circular reasoning

2. I heard about a woman who got some of the money and didn't return it. The next day she fell and broke her leg. Then she knew she had done the wrong thing.

   ____

3. Insurance companies always cheat people. My insurance company took advantage of me once.

   ____

4. Picking up the money that fell onto the road is similar to picking flowers that grow in the forest.

   ____

5. The motorists who stopped to take the money should not be prosecuted for stealing. They didn't cause the accident.

   ____

2 Revising for Content Review your letter for faulty reasoning and make any necessary corrections.

Strategy

Correcting Spelling Errors

Always edit your writing for spelling errors. When you do, review the spelling rules in Appendix 1, but remember that you can't always count on rules to help you with spelling. You will often have to use a dictionary to check words you are not sure you have spelled correctly.

WRITING WITH COMPUTERS

Most word processing programs will check your spelling for you. However, you still must proofread. If you misspell a word and the misspelling creates another word, the spelling checker will not catch it. Look at the example below. Which word is incorrect? Will the spelling checker mark it incorrect? Why or why not?

We saw there car in the street.

3 Identifying and Correcting Spelling Errors Correct the words below if they are incorrect, or write *correct* if there is no mistake. Use your dictionary if you are not sure.

1. successful	*correct*	**6.** estimatted	________
2. moralety	________	**7.** defendant	________
3. evil	________	**8.** prosecutor	________
4. honnestly	________	**9.** government	________
5. truely	________	**10.** taxs	________

CORRECTING HYPHENATION ERRORS

Even though the computer will hyphenate words for you automatically, hyphenation is still a useful skill to know.

General Rules for Hyphenation

1. If a word is too long to fit at the end of the line, divide it between syllables and put the second part of the word on the next line.
2. Don't divide words that have one syllable.
3. Divide words after prefixes or before suffixes.
   con-struc-tion   em-bez-zle-ment   com-fort-a-ble
4. Divide words between two consonants.
   col-lege   ad-dic-tion   com-pul-sive
5. If you are not sure how to divide a word, check your dictionary.
   Look at these examples:

Incorrect	**Correct**
■ We couldn't find the pla- ce they told us about.	■ We couldn't find the place they told us about.
■ He's always borr- owing money.	■ He's always borrow- ing money.

4 Hyphenating If the following words didn't fit at the end of a line, how would you divide them? Draw a line between where you could correctly hyphenate them.

1. expen/sive
2. accounting
3. irrelevant
4. organization
5. consumer
6. generous
7. argument
8. immoral

5 Editing for Form Edit the following paragraph for form. Find nineteen spelling errors, four hyphenation errors, and three comma splices.

March 17, 20___

Dear Editor,

I am a student at Pacific College, and I think the school spends too much money on activitys that are not related to educattion. One of the bigest expenses is athletics, for example, it has to pay for coache-s' saliries, equipment, and building stadiems. It also sponsors a free stude-nt newspaper and many student activaties such as partys, plays, and conserts.

Many staf members spend a lot of time organizing and planing these activities, they have to be paid salaries for this work as well. These activatys are fine, but not when the college is decresing libery hours on the weekends and increasing class size, I like football games, part-ys, and conserts, but I beleive that my educattion is more important.

Sincerely,

A concerned studnet

▲ Some colleges and universities spend a lot of money on sports programs.

Evaluating Your Writing

6 Using a Rubric Read the rubric below with your class. Then use the rubric to score your letter.

Score	Description
3 **Excellent**	■ **Content:** Letter presents a clear opinion and supports the writer's point of view with reasons that aren't faulty, examples, and/or predictions. ■ **Organization:** Paragraph ideas are introduced by a topic sentence. Opinions are grouped with supporting statements. ■ **Vocabulary:** Vocabulary is specific, varied, and used correctly throughout. ■ **Grammar:** Modals and *if*-clauses are used correctly. There are very few grammar mistakes, and the meaning of the letter is clear and easy to understand. ■ **Spelling and Mechanics:** Most words are spelled correctly, and punctuation is correct. Correct hyphenation and letter form are used.
2 **Adequate**	■ **Content:** Letter presents a clear opinion. One or two reasons, examples, and/or predictions may be unclear, or the reader may have questions. ■ **Organization:** Paragraph ideas are introduced by a topic sentence. Some opinions may not be grouped with supporting statements. ■ **Vocabulary:** Vocabulary is specific and varied, but some words may be used incorrectly. ■ **Grammar:** Most modals and *if*-clauses are used correctly. There are some grammar mistakes, but the meaning of the letter is clear. ■ **Spelling and Mechanics:** Letter includes some spelling and/or punctuation mistakes. There may be some mistakes in letter form.
1 **Developing**	■ **Content:** Letter does not present much information about the writer's opinion. Letter includes very few reasons to support opinion, or support is confusing. ■ **Organization:** Paragraphs may not have a topic sentence. Opinions are not grouped with supporting statements. ■ **Vocabulary:** Vocabulary is limited, and/or there are too many mistakes to understand the ideas. ■ **Grammar:** Letter contains many grammar problems that are confusing to the reader. ■ **Spelling and Mechanics:** Letter contains many distracting spelling and/or punctuation mistakes. Correct letter form is not used.

7 **Peer Sharing** Exchange letters with a classmate whose opinion is different from yours. Read his or her letter, and discuss the reasons for your different opinions.

8 **Writing the Second Draft** Rewrite your letter using your rubric evaluation. Revise for content, and edit for form. Then give your letter to your teacher for comments. When your teacher returns your paper, ask him or her about any comments you don't understand.

Part 4 Expansion Activities

What Do You Think?

Evaluating Arguments for Faulty Reasoning
Practice evaluating arguments. Listen to a talk show program on the radio or TV, or read a letter to the editor in a newspaper. Take notes on the person's argument. In groups, discuss whether the person used faulty reasoning.

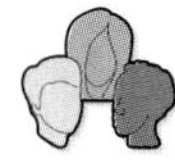

1 **Sharing Your Writing** Tape your letters to the board in two groups: one group for letters saying that the people should give the money back, and another group for the letters saying that the people shouldn't. Go to the board and read some of the letters. Answer these questions:

1. What reasons were given for each opinion?
2. Are you and your classmates in general agreement, or are there many differing opinions?
3. What are the main reasons for the differences of opinion?

2 **Debating the Issue** Your teacher will split the class in two teams based on the opinions you expressed in your letters. Students on both teams take turns presenting the reasons for their opinions. Then both teams give their counterarguments. Finally, each team sums up.

3 **Evaluating Letters to the Editor** Look at a local, international, or school newspaper or magazine. Find the letters to the editor. Often some are logical and others are emotional; some are serious and others try to be funny. Which letters do you like? Why? Do they give strong or moderate opinions?

4 Writing a Letter to the Editor

Find an article or letter in a newspaper or on the Internet, and write a letter in response to it.

5 Writing in Your Journal

Choose one of the following activities:

1. Write a letter to your teacher telling him or her what you like about the writing course and what you have learned. Then write a suggestion you have for improving the course. You can give this to your teacher if you like.
2. Write your reaction to one of the proverbs or sayings on page 44 or to another one that you know.
3. Write the word *BUSINESS* in the center of a page. Then quickly, without thinking, write around it any words, phrases, or ideas you associate with the word. Use some of these words or ideas to write about your opinion of business.
4. Read a newspaper article, and write a reaction to it.

6 Researching Ethics Questions

There are many sites on the Internet that consider ethics questions. *Ethics* refers to decisions regarding right and wrong behavior. Some common ethical problems concern lying, cheating, and stealing.

In groups, read the ethics questions below. Using the words in parentheses, search the Internet for websites that deal with ethics and these specific issues. Use the information you find to help you answer the questions. Discuss your answers with the class.

1. Your best friend is failing math. The two of you have planned a vacation together, but if he fails, he won't be able to go. He has asked you to help him on a test. You don't want him to fail, but you have never cheated before. What should you do?
   Search ideas: (*cheat* + *test* + *ethics*)
2. You see your best friend's boyfriend or girlfriend out with someone else. If you say anything, your friend will be hurt, but doesn't he or she have the right to know?
   Search ideas: (*cheat* + *best friend* + *ethics* + *boyfriend* or *girlfriend*)
3. You know that your best friend is shoplifting (stealing from stores). You are worried that he or she is going to get into trouble. You have tried to talk about this problem, but it didn't help. What should you do?
   Search ideas: (*shoplifting* + *steal* + *ethics*)

Self-Assessment Log

In this chapter, you worked through the activities listed below. How much did they help you to become a better writer? Check *A lot, A little,* or *Not at all.*

	A lot	**A little**	**Not at all**
I used free writing to generate ideas.	❑	❑	❑
I read and discussed a web page article.	❑	❑	❑
I practiced writing my opinion.	❑	❑	❑
I learned to express obligation and give advice with modals.	❑	❑	❑
I learned to support an opinion with a general statement and examples.	❑	❑	❑
I learned to support an opinion with a prediction.	❑	❑	❑
I learned to avoid faulty reasoning.	❑	❑	❑
I used a writing rubric to evaluate my first draft.	❑	❑	❑
(Add something) ______________________________ ______________________________	❑	❑	❑

Jobs and Professions

In This Chapter

Genre Focus: Narrative

Writing Product

An autobiographical narrative paragraph

Writing Process

- Learn effective ways to describe accomplishments.
- Use a spider map to organize information.
- Limit information in a paragraph.
- Write a concluding sentence.
- Use the simple past and the present perfect tenses.
- Use the present perfect continuous.
- Use demonstratives to unify a paragraph.

"The secret of achievement is to hold a picture of a successful outcome in mind."

—Henry David Thoreau
American writer, philosopher, and naturalist (1817–1862)

Connecting to the Topic

1. What accomplishment does the photograph show?
2. What has been your greatest accomplishment in life? How did you feel at the time?
3. What are some things you would like to accomplish?

Part 1 Before You Write

Exploring Ideas

Strategy

Describing Your Accomplishments

In this chapter, you are going to write a paragraph in response to the following question on a job or college application:

Describe an accomplishment in your life.

On application forms (and during interviews), you may be asked to describe a personal accomplishment. In discussing personal accomplishments, you want to show that you are special or different in some way. Be positive and focus on your good points. It's important to describe qualities that would show you could succeed at the job or college for which you are applying.

1 Discussing Accomplishments Following are some sample instructions for a college or job application. Below are some examples of conversations people might have about answering such questions. In small groups, discuss the reactions of the students in the pictures below.

- What have you accomplished in the past two years?
- Tell us something about yourself that will help us know you better.
- Write a short personal history.
- Write about the most difficult thing you have ever done.
- Discuss your duties in your previous or present job.

I've only been hanging out and playing my guitar. I can't write about that!
And I've been spending all my time in English class. I don't have time for anything else.

I hate filling out these applications! I never know what to say about myself!
But you've accomplished a lot during the last two years. You immigrated to the States, you're learning English, and you had a baby!

I have to fill out this job application. What can I say about my part-time job at Mc-Farland's Fast Foods?
I don't want to brag about my scholarship.

2 Discussing Appropriateness of Topics In small groups, discuss the following questions: In your country, is it impolite to talk about your successes in an interview? Are there any topics you should avoid (for example, religion or politics)? Why should you avoid them?

Building Vocabulary

3 Discussing Vocabulary Words The words and phrases below describe personal characteristics. In small groups, discuss their meanings. Put a check mark (✔) next to the positive words. Put an X next to the negative words. Look up any words you don't know.

☑	ambitious	☐	a good sense of humor
☐	sociable	☐	self-confident
☐	creative	☐	agreeable
☐	disciplined	☐	moody
☐	enthusiastic	☐	untrustworthy
☐	hardworking	☐	cold
☐	jealous	☐	sensitive
☐	aggressive	☐	generous
☐	selfless	☐	irresponsible
☐	difficult	☐	optimistic

USING ANTONYMS

Some antonyms (words that have opposite meaning) are completely different words.

Example

difficult—easy-going

Some antonyms are different forms of the same word.

Example

attractive—unattractive

Many of these types of antonyms are formed with *un,* a prefix that means *not.*

4 Writing Antonyms On a separate piece of paper, write antonyms for the adjectives listed in Activity 3. Use a dictionary to check your work.

WRITING WITH COMPUTERS

If your word processing program does not include a dictionary, look for one online. Do an online search for **dictionary** + **English** and you will find many.

Strategy

Making Direct Statements and Implying

One way to write about yourself is to state directly that you have a specific quality or talent, and then illustrate it with a specific example in order to *show* that you have that quality or talent.

Another way to write about yourself is to imply—that is, suggest indirectly—that you have a certain quality or talent by describing an accomplishment that illustrates that quality or talent. For example, you might want to imply that you have qualities such as intelligence, honesty, creativity, or humor. If you show how you solved a difficult problem, for example, the reader can make the inference that you are smart and creative.

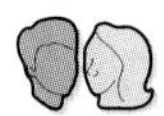

What Do You Think?

Describing Qualities and Talents

Practice thinking of ways to illustrate particular qualities. Work with a partner. Together, think of situations that would show the following qualities in a person:

intelligence	courage	sense of humor
patience	honesty	creativity

5 Evaluating Accomplishments

In small groups, choose three of the people described below and on page 69, and discuss how their experience and accomplishments show that they have characteristics that are important to succeed in work and school. Name those characteristics.

▲ Paolo taught himself to play the guitar.

1. Miguel's mother works afternoons, so Miguel has taken care of his younger brother after school for the last four years.
2. Paolo taught himself how to play the guitar and plays in a band.
3. Greta works as a salesclerk in her uncle's store.
4. Shenner has been studying English for the last nine months with money he got from a scholarship for being the top student in his class.
5. Yoshi likes to create computer games.

6. Ana is a cyclist and takes long trips on her bicycle.
7. Sophia has been raising three children for the last eight years.
8. All of Parvin's friends tell her their problems.

6 Discussing Your Accomplishments

In the same group, discuss one or two accomplishments or experiences you could write about on a job or college application form. How does the experience show you have qualities that are important for success? Which qualities does the experience illustrate?

7 Writing about Your Accomplishments

Write notes about the experience or accomplishment you think illustrates your best qualities. Answer these questions:

1. What did you do?
2. What was difficult about the experience?
3. How did you face the difficulty?
4. What qualities does the experience show you have?
5. In what ways are these qualities important to succeeding in school or work?
6. What did you accomplish through the experience?

Organizing Ideas

Strategy

Using Graphic Organizers

A spider map is a type of graphic organizer that allows you to develop several different aspects of one central concept or idea. For instance, if you were trying to brainstorm ideas about your accomplishments, you could use different sections of a spider map to list ideas for different types of accomplishments: academic, financial, personal, and work-related. After you've brainstormed ideas, you can see the ideas that will be the best to develop in your writing. The sections that have the most information will likely be the easiest and most interesting to write about.

8 **Analyzing a Graphic Organizer** Look at the spider map below. Which aspect(s) of the writer's life should this student write about on a college application? Why?

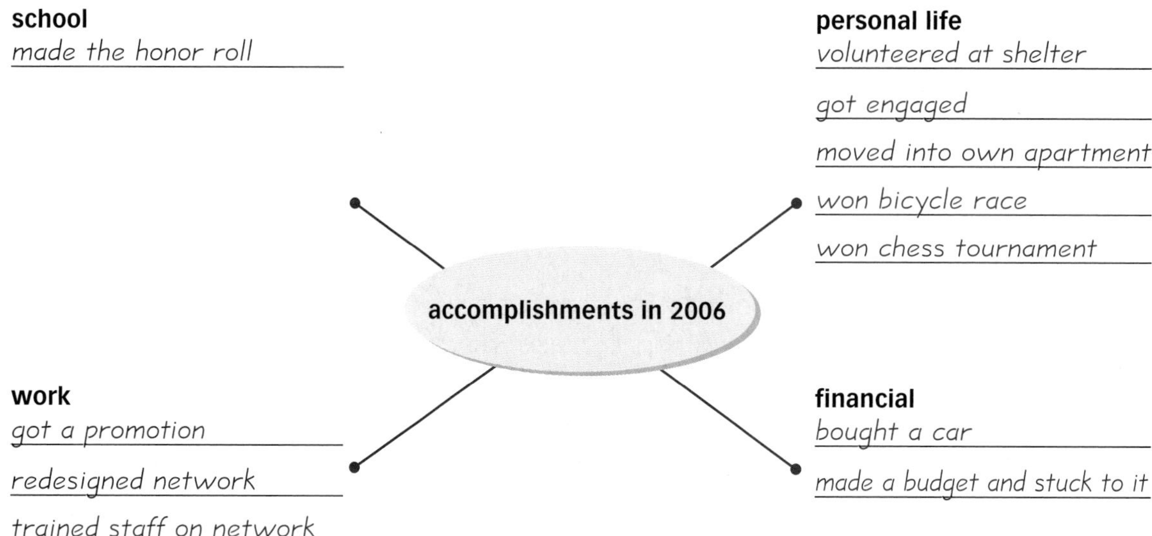

9 **Creating a Graphic Organizer** Draw a spider map. Use the map above as a model. Choose four aspects of your life and brainstorm your accomplishments for each section.

10 **Limiting Information** Below is a response to the prompt, *Describe an accomplishment that shows you have the qualities needed to succeed in college.* Read the paragraph, and cross out any information you think the writer should leave out. Share your ideas with a partner.

I have many qualities that have made me a success as a bike messenger. First of all, I have the ability to persevere when there are difficulties. I also find math very difficult, but I have a tutor now who has been a great help to me. And bike messengers run into many difficulties. I have had problems with drivers who almost run me over, constant rain for weeks at a time, unreadable addresses, and rude customers. I think the drivers in New York are the worst in any city I have seen. In addition, my dedication to the job has also served me well. I believe that you should do your best at even the most routine jobs. For example, I work hard at finding short cuts around the city. And I'm proud to say that when a package needs to be delivered really quickly, my boss always calls on me. Finally, my success as a bike messenger is partly due to my sense of humor. Many times I have wanted to quit, but I just try to laugh at the situation.

Strategy

Using More Than One Paragraph

You will probably be able to write about your experience in one paragraph. However, if the experience has several parts, you might want to use two paragraphs. For example, you might write in one paragraph about how you worked when your job was starting, and in the second paragraph about how you changed to face a problem you were experiencing. Remember that each paragraph should have its own topic sentence.

Writing Topic Sentences

The topic sentence for each paragraph should make the reader interested in reading more. It should grab the reader's attention and be positive. The reader should know immediately that the paragraph is going to be about an experience or accomplishment that illustrates your strengths and good qualities. All of the sentences in the paragraph should relate to the topic sentence.

11 Choosing the Best Topic Sentences The following are topic sentences for paragraphs about an accomplishment. Discuss them in small groups. Which ones do you like? Why?

1. I have always danced just for fun, but I recently realized that dancing has helped me develop three important qualities.
2. I guess a lot of people take care of their children, so it isn't very special.
3. Two years ago, my family and I immigrated to Vancouver, Canada, and my life changed dramatically.
4. A very important thing has been happening.
5. Although I was born in Vietnam, I have been living in a small town in Texas for the last three years, and the two cultures have affected me in many important ways.
6. My relationship with my children has developed my creativity, discipline, and sense of humor.
7. Last year I had a very bad experience.
8. I like to go swimming a lot.

12 Writing a Draft Topic Sentence Write a draft topic sentence for your paragraph.

Strategy

Writing Concluding Sentences

Your paragraph will need a concluding sentence. As you learned in a previous chapter, a good concluding sentence can do many things, including summarize the main points of your paragraph. In addition, for a paragraph about an accomplishment, the concluding sentence can:

- tell what you learned about yourself from the experience you chose.
- describe a hope for the future.
- state that the accomplishment you described shows that you will succeed at the job or school to which you are applying.

13 Choosing the Best Concluding Sentences Discuss the following concluding sentences in small groups. Which ones are effective? Why? Which ones are not? Why not?

1. I guess raising children isn't easy for anyone.
2. I can never do things I don't enjoy, but when I like something, I work pretty hard at it.
3. I hope that my experience raising my own children will help me be a better teacher.
4. I feel that I've experienced the best of both cultures, and I hope to use this experience in my future work.
5. I never want to go through such a horrible experience again.
6. Now I know that if I enjoy something and know it is important, I can work really hard to make it a success.

14 Discussing Possible Concluding Sentences In small groups, tell the other students what experience you are going to write about. Discuss some possible concluding sentences you might use.

◄ Raising children is challenging and rewarding.

Part 2 Developing Writing Skills

Developing Cohesion and Clarity

USING THE CORRECT TENSE: SIMPLE PAST OR PRESENT PERFECT

Simple Past Tense

Use the past tense to describe an action or state that was completed in the past, especially when the specific time is mentioned.

Example

I was in Beirut in 2005. (The state is completed and the time period is mentioned.)

Present Perfect Tense

Use the present perfect tense to describe an action or state that was completed in the past but we don't know when.

Example

I have been to Beirut many times. (We don't know when.)

Use the present perfect tense to describe an action that was started in the past and continues to the present. In this case, *for* or *since* is often used.

Examples

Every year since 2002, I have gone to Beirut for summer vacation. (I still go.)

I have lived in St. Petersburg for three years. (I still live there.)

1 Completing Sentences with the Correct Verb Form

Complete the sentences below with the simple past or present perfect form of the verb in parentheses.

▲ Maria has studied dancing for many years.

Examples

(You live in Tokyo now.) I *have lived* (live) in Tokyo for three years.

(You live in New York now.) I *lived* (live) in Cairo for three years.

1. My father ________________ (come) to visit me once a year since 1997.
2. My mother ________________ (come) to visit me every year since I arrived.
3. I ________________ (have) two jobs this year.
4. I ________________ (have) two jobs last year.
5. I ________________ (learn) a lot when I was waiting to immigrate.

6. I ____________________ (learn) a lot in my life.
7. I ____________________ (work) in this store for a month now.
8. I ____________________ (work) in that store for a month, but then I quit.
9. Kelsey ____________________ (take) dance classes last year.
10. She ____________________ (take) dance classes for one year.
11. Rashad ____________________ (be) to Mexico City many times since 2000.
12. He ____________________ (go) to Morocco two years ago.

USING THE CORRECT TENSE: PRESENT PERFECT AND PRESENT PERFECT CONTINUOUS

Present Perfect

The present perfect tense describes actions and states that were completed at an unspecified time in the past or continue to the present.

Examples

I have been to San Francisco. (Completed in the past. The time is not specified.)
I have lived in San Francisco for three years. (Continues to the present.)

The following time expressions often appear with the present perfect tense: *already, just, recently, still, yet, twice, three (four, etc.) times, for,* and *since.*

Examples

I have visited San Francisco three times.
My parents have just returned from Europe.

Present Perfect Continuous

The present perfect continuous tense describes an event or state that is currently in progress as well as *how long* it has been in progress up until now.

The following time expressions often appear with it: *so far, up to now, for* (a period of time), or *since* (a beginning time).

Examples

I have been going to that restaurant for months.
We have been swimming a lot this summer.

Present Perfect versus Present Perfect Continuous

Don't use the present perfect continuous with most nonaction verbs—verbs that express feelings, opinions, possession, or perceptions. Instead, use the present perfect tense.

The following are examples of nonaction verbs: *be, believe, know, like, need, prefer, seem, realize,* and *want.*

Possession: *belong to, have, own, possess*
Perceptions: *smell, look, taste, see*

Examples

They have known about this meeting since last month.

I haven't seen her for years.

A few verbs, such as *live, make, study, think,* and *work,* are used with the present perfect continuous or the present perfect with little difference in meaning when a time expression is used.

Examples

She has worked at this company for five years.

She has been working at this company for five years.

We have lived here since 1998.

We have been living here since 1998.

---

2 Completing Sentences with the Correct Verb Form

Complete the sentences with the present perfect or present perfect continuous form of the verbs in parentheses.

Examples

I *have known* (know) about this for a long time.

I *have been thinking* (think) about this since yesterday.

1. I ____________ (work) at many different restaurants, but the Starlight Diner is my favorite.
2. Has he ever ____________ (work) in a restaurant?
3. I ____________ (not write) my essay yet.
4. They ____________ (paint) the house for a month, and they still aren't finished.
5. She ____________ already ____________ (fill out) her application.
6. She ____________ (fill out) her application for the last four hours.
7. Marco is always late. I ____________ (wait) for him many times.
8. He's late again today. ____________ (wait) for him for two hours!
9. I ____________ (do) calligraphy for four years now.

3 Completing a Paragraph with the Correct Verb Forms

Complete the paragraphs below with the simple past, present perfect, or present perfect continuous forms of the verbs in parentheses. Sometimes both present perfect and present perfect continuous are correct.

I ___have liked___ (1) (like) to write since I ________ (2) (be) five years old. When I first ________ (3) (hold) a pen in my hand and carefully ________ (4) (draw) the beautiful Japanese characters, I ________ (5) (know) I ________ (6) (want) to be a writer. Ever since that day, I ________ (7) (write) in my free time. When I ________ (8) (come) to Miami six months ago to study English, I ________ (9) (not realize) I would feel so frustrated. I ________ (10) (have) the thoughts of a 19-year-old but the writing skills of a three-year-old!

Although I ________ (11) (study) hard since that day, I still ________ (12) (not write) an essay in English I can be proud of. This experience ________ (13) (be) frustrating, but I ________ (14) (learn) a lot from it. For six months, I ________ (15) (experience) the world through the words of another culture. I ________ (16) (learn) different ways of communicating and can use these new methods in my writing in Japanese.

TOEFL® IBT

Focus on Testing

Checking for Correct Tense

When you are writing a paragraph under pressure in a testing situation, take time to make sure each verb form is in the correct tense. After you've finished writing, reread your paragraph from the beginning. First, make sure the overall time frame is correct; for example, if you're talking about a past event, most verbs in the paragraph should be in some form of the past. Then locate the verb in each sentence. Ask yourself if it is in the correct form. Also, look for time expressions in each sentence (such as *since* or *for*) that might require a particular tense.

Practice Give yourself 5 minutes to look for and correct verb tense errors in the following paragraph. Read the whole paragraph before you make changes. Do not look up any information.

My life was very easy until I was 15 years old. My family was rich, and I never worry about anything. Then one day my father left us. We sell our beautiful house and moved to a small apartment. My mother has to go to work in an office. My brothers and sisters and I have left private school and began attending public school. I was extremely lonely and unhappy. I couldn't make friends at the new school. Everyone thought I was a snob. My life has changed when I got an after school job at a small bakery in town. The owner, Mrs. Garcia, took a special interest in me. She has taught me all about baking, running a small business, and life in general. Two years ago, Mrs. Garcia retired. Since that time, I have been running the bakery on my own. It hasn't been easy to run a business and attend school part-time. I've had to work very hard, but it has been worth it. I can truthfully say that I've been experiencing an easy life and a hard life and, in many ways, the hard life is better.

USING DEMONSTRATIVES TO UNIFY A PARAGRAPH

A good writer uses phrases with *this, that, these,* or *those*—demonstratives—to refer to ideas in previous sentences.

Use *that* or *those* when referring to things and experiences in the past.

Example

When I was 15, I read a book about Sammy Sosa. <u>That</u> was the first time I thought about becoming a professional baseball player.

Use *this* or *these* when referring to things and experiences that are still relevant today.

Example

My classmates and I have gotten very close. <u>These</u> students have taught me that language doesn't have to be a barrier to friendship.

The following examples include a demonstrative that refers to an experience in the past that is still relevant today.

Examples

Before my grandmother went with me to the airport, she told me to work hard and not to forget my family. <u>Those</u> were her last words to me. I never saw her again. However, I will pass <u>this</u> lesson on to my children.

Those is used to refer to the words spoken in the past.
This is used to refer to the lesson that is still relevant today.

Examples

Five years ago, I was failing math and thinking about quitting school. Luckily, my teacher spent a lot of time working with me. Eventually I passed with a *B*. <u>That</u> experience taught me about perseverance and hard work. I still value <u>these</u> qualities.

That is used to refer to an experience that occurred in the past.
These is used to refer to qualities that are relevant today.

4 Identifying Demonstratives Underline the phrases with demonstratives in Activity 3 on page 76. What words or ideas do they refer to?

5 Completing Sentences with Demonstratives Complete the sentences below with *this, that, these,* or *those.*

1. I first began to play soccer when I was four years old, and I have spent some of my happiest moments since *that* ________ time on the soccer field.
2. A very important holiday in China is New Year's Day. On ________ day, we have a big feast.
3. My favorite aunt died recently. ________ experience was sad and frightening because no one close to me had ever died before. However, it has made me see life differently.
4. I have learned French, Hungarian, and Spanish, and I'm now learning English. I love the different qualities of each of ________ languages.
5. When I was a teenager, I had to work nights and weekends to help my mother pay for food, rent, and other necessities. ________ years were very difficult for us, but they taught me to be a hard worker.

6 Completing Sentences with Prepositional Phrases and Demonstratives You can use prepositions and prepositional phrases with demonstratives to help unify a paragraph. Add one of the following phrases to the second sentence in each of the numbered items below. Use a demonstrative *(this, that, these,* or *those)* in each phrase.

for ________ reason	in ________ school
on ________ day	because of ________ factors
in ________ city	during ________ years

1. Two years and six months ago, my first child was born. *On that day,* ________ my life changed.
2. I lived in a refugee camp in Thailand from the age of seven to eleven. ________, my parents' only hope was going to live in North America.
3. I have always been shy. ________, learning a new language is a challenge for me.
4. I came to Mexico City two years ago. ________ I have had many new experiences.

5. I was too short and was not thin enough. ____________________, I could not continue to dance professionally.

6. I came to the International English Program six months ago. ____________________, I have made many new friends.

7 Writing the First Draft Write your paragraph. Write about an accomplishment or experience that shows you have the qualities to succeed in a particular job or educational program. Use the ideas you developed in the beginning of the chapter. Don't forget to include:

- a topic sentence.
- demonstratives such as *this, that, these,* and *those.*
- a concluding sentence.

Part 3 Revising and Editing

1 Revising for Content Read the following paragraph. Cross out irrelevant ideas, and identify where you could connect ideas to make the paragraph shorter and more cohesive.

I have been taking an English class for the last six months. This has been a rewarding but difficult change in my life. Before that, I spent all my time raising my family, a daughter who is now five and a son who is three. My daughter's name is Karen. She is in kindergarten, and my son now goes to day care. Because I did not speak much English, my focus was my home and my neighborhood, where I felt comfortable and could speak Spanish. I spoke only Spanish at home and in my neighborhood. When I needed to take my children to the doctor or speak with my landlord, my younger sisters translated for me. One of them would go with me and speak to the doctor in English and then tell me what he said in Spanish. Now I have become more independent. I have learned a lot from my classmates, and I have also realized that as a mother I have had many experiences that they are interested in. Now my sisters tell me to speak to the doctor or landlord myself. I go to stores where I have to speak English, and I speak English in the clinic where I take my son to the doctor. This was very difficult at first, but I have been feeling more and more comfortable about my ability to communicate with other English speakers. I hope to use this new confidence to get a job.

2 **Editing for Form** Review the rules for capitalization in Appendix 2. Correct the capitalization in the sentences below. If the sentence is correct, write *no mistake* next to it.

1. Because my Mother doesn't speak ~~e~~English, I have to translate for her.
2. When I first moved to the southwest, I got a job as a Salesperson.
3. I have lived in miami, Los Angeles, and dallas.
4. I received a Scholarship from Grant college in the Spring and started classes in september.
5. This semester I am taking Math, physics, english, and Government.

3 **Correcting Verb Forms** All of the underlined words and phrases in the following paragraph contain errors. Read through the entire paragraph. Then read it again and correct the mistakes.

Some children play sports; others collect stamps. However, since I [1] <u>~~has given~~</u> *was* young, my hobby was owning my own business. I [2] <u>has given</u> very good in mathematics, so when I [3] <u>was having fifteen</u>, I [4] <u>start</u> a tutoring business. Every afternoon after school I [5] <u>am teaching</u> math to younger children. I had fun, and the students did too. That experience [6] <u>has given</u> me confidence. In 2005, I [7] <u>have entered</u> the university and started another business. I [8] <u>taught</u> businesspeople how to use different computer programs. That business [9] <u>was being</u> very successful. At first, I [10] <u>am spending</u> all of my free time at my business. That [11] <u>is</u> a mistake. The first year, I failed three classes. That showed me that you can't do everything alone. Then I [12] <u>have hire</u> two assistants. Now my business [13] <u>was</u> doing well and my classes [14] <u>is</u> too.

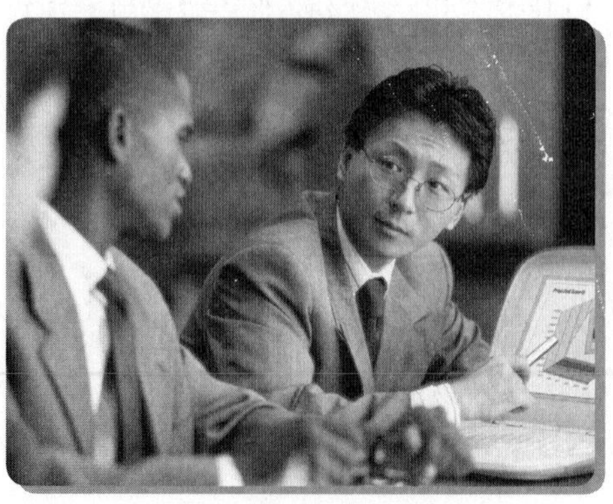

◄ Technology has dramatically changed the way companies do business.

Evaluating Your Writing

4 Using a Rubric Read the rubric below with your class. Then use the rubric to score your paragraph.

Score	Description
3 **Excellent**	■ **Content:** Paragraph describes an accomplishment and illustrates the writer's qualities. ■ **Organization:** Paragraph ideas are introduced by a positive and interesting topic sentence. Concluding sentence is reflective or looks into the future. Paragraph doesn't contain irrelevant information. ■ **Vocabulary:** Vocabulary is specific, varied, and used correctly throughout. ■ **Grammar:** Verb forms are correct, and demonstratives (*this, that, these, those*) and prepositional phrases are used correctly. ■ **Spelling and Mechanics:** Most words are spelled correctly (especially past participles), and capitalization is correct.
2 **Adequate**	■ **Content:** Paragraph describes an accomplishment, but it's not clear what qualities the accomplishment is supposed to illustrate. ■ **Organization:** There is a topic sentence, and the following sentences are relevant. There is a concluding sentence. One idea may be irrelevant. ■ **Vocabulary:** Vocabulary is somewhat varied. There may be one or two usage errors. ■ **Grammar:** Verb forms are mostly correct. Demonstratives (*this, that, these, those*) and prepositional phrases are used but may contain some mistakes. ■ **Spelling and Mechanics:** There may be some spelling and capitalization mistakes.
1 **Developing**	■ **Content:** Paragraph does not describe an accomplishment or illustrate the writer's qualities. ■ **Organization:** Paragraph ideas do not connect to the topic sentence, or there is no topic sentence. There is no concluding sentence. There is a lot of irrelevant information. ■ **Vocabulary:** Vocabulary is limited, or there are too many mistakes to understand or follow the ideas. ■ **Grammar:** There are many verb form errors. Demonstratives (*this, that, these, those*) and prepositional phrases are not used. ■ **Spelling and Mechanics:** Many distracting spelling and capitalization mistakes.

5 Writing the Second Draft Rewrite your paragraph using your rubric evaluation. Revise for content, and edit for form. Then give your paper to your teacher for comments. When your teacher returns your paper, ask him or her about any comments you don't understand.

Part 4 Expansion Activities

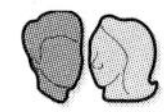

1 Interviewing a Classmate Pretend to interview another student for a job or school. Find out what school or job she or he would like to apply for. Read your partner's paragraph and ask for more information about the accomplishment. Then ask other questions such as the following:

1. Why did you choose your major field of study?
2. What subjects in school have you liked the most/least? Why?
3. Tell me about your duties in past jobs.
4. Have you ever done any volunteer work? What kind and why?
5. Why are you interested in this position/school?
6. Where do you see yourself in five years?

2 Assessing Your Progress Answer these questions about your writing:

1. What have you learned so far in this course?
2. How do you feel about writing?
3. What do you like most about writing?
4. What do you like least about writing?

3 Writing a Personal History Some applications ask for an autobiography or a personal history. Expand the paragraph you wrote for this section into several paragraphs. End with a paragraph describing your future goals.

4 **Writing in Your Journal** Write in your journal about the following topics:

1. Qualities that you wish you had and experiences you think would help you develop those qualities in yourself
2. A job you'd love to have, the qualities you need to succeed at this job, and the experiences or accomplishments in your life that illustrate these qualities

5 **Researching Tips for Job Hunters** Many websites include information to help you write about and discuss your personal and professional accomplishments. Work in groups. Use the words below to research two or three tips or helpful suggestions for writing resumes and talking about your accomplishments and experience. Share the information you find with your class.

success + job + accomplishments + application

Self-Assessment Log

In this chapter, you worked through the activities listed below. How much did they help you to become a better writer? Check *A lot, A little,* or *Not at all.*

	A lot	A little	Not at all
I learned effective ways to describe my accomplishments.	❑	❑	❑
I used a spider map to organize my ideas.	❑	❑	❑
I practiced limiting information in a paragraph.	❑	❑	❑
I practiced writing concluding sentences.	❑	❑	❑
I used the simple past and present perfect tenses.	❑	❑	❑
I used the present perfect continuous tense.	❑	❑	❑
I used demonstratives to unify a paragraph.	❑	❑	❑
I used a writing rubric to evaluate my first draft.	❑	❑	❑
(Add something) ______________________	❑	❑	❑
______________________			

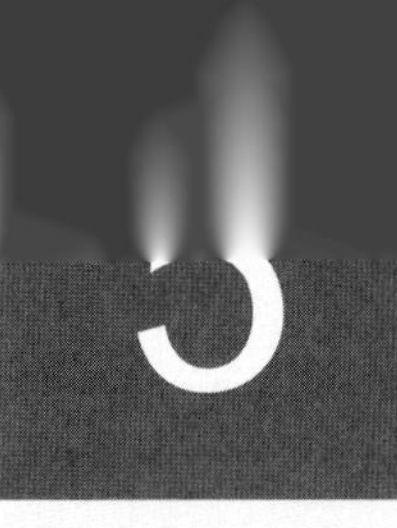

Lifestyles Around the World

In This Chapter

Genre Focus: Narrative

Writing Product

A two-paragraph narrative about a personal experience

Writing Process

- Identify and discuss the moral of a story.
- Use a graphic organizer to plan a narrative.
- Identify where to start a second paragraph in a narrative.
- Use details to enhance the reader's experience.
- Use the past perfect tense.
- Identify and omit digressions.

"Progress comes from the intelligent use of experience."

—Elbert Hubbard
American writer and philosopher (1856-1915)

Connecting to the Topic

1. What traditional activity does the picture show?
2. Would you ever take part in this activity? Why or why not?
3. If you lived in Spain, would your answer to number 2 be different? Why or why not?

Part 1 Before You Write

Exploring Ideas

1 Discussing Lessons Learned from Experience Read the list of lessons below—things that people might learn from experience. In small groups, discuss the list. Discuss experiences that might teach someone each of the lessons. Do you agree with the statements?

1. It's important to think for yourself.
2. Self-discipline is an essential quality.
3. Sometimes you have to take risks to get something you want.
4. Friendship is one of the most valuable things in life.
5. You should never make promises you can't keep.
6. If you want a good relationship, you have to compromise.
7. Sometimes parents really do know best.
8. Sometimes it's best to lie to the people you love.
9. Hard work can be satisfying.
10. The only thing that's certain is change.
11. It's great to be independent.

Boy! Life sure will be different . . . .

2 Inventing a Story About a Lesson Learned Look at the pictures below, and make up a story for one of them. The story should be about how the person in the picture learned an important lesson. Share your story with your group.

Well . . .
But then again . . . .

My own place . . .

Don't worry . . .

3 **Free Writing** Free write about a lesson from the list in Activity 1 or another lesson. Write for ten minutes about the experience that taught you that lesson. Don't worry about correctness or organization now.

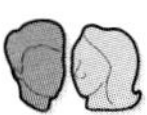

What Do You Think?

Identifying the Moral of a Story

With a partner, take turns telling a fairy tale, a fable, or a children's story. Let your partner guess the moral. Talk about how the story teaches a lesson by answering the following questions:

1. Who is the main character?
2. What is he or she like?
3. What happens to the main character?
4. Does he or she change? How?

Building Vocabulary

4 **Using a Vocabulary Chart** Below are some words that you might use to write about important life lessons. Work in small groups to complete the chart. Add words that you learned in your discussion or used in your free write.

Nouns	Verbs	Adjectives
decision	change	independent
friendship	compromise	valuable
importance	lie	*decisive*
promise	risk	
self-discipline		

5 Using New Vocabulary Divide into two teams. Each team will try to get the other to answer a question that demonstrates the meaning of a word in the chart in Activity 4.

WRITING WITH COMPUTERS
Most word processing programs contain a thesaurus. A thesaurus gives you the synonyms and antonyms of a specific word. Because many words have a number of slightly different meanings, you must choose a word that has the exact meaning you want. Then look it up in the dictionary to make sure it's the right word.

Examples

Name someone who is decisive.
Name something that is valuable or something people value.
Who risks their lives or money?
What is an example of self-discipline?
Whom do you make promises to?

Organizing Ideas

Strategy

Using a Graphic Organizer to Write an Anecdote

An anecdote is a short description of an interesting event that really happened. Writers use anecdotes to illustrate or explain ideas. Paragraphs used in telling anecdotes or stories are organized chronologically.

In this chapter, you are going to write an autobiographical narrative: two paragraphs that tell an anecdote about something that happened to you that taught you a lesson about life. Your anecdote should answer the following questions:

1. When and where did the event take place?
2. Who was involved?
3. What happened?
4. Why did it happen?
5. What was the result?
6. What was the lesson you learned?

A graphic organizer, like the one on the next page can help you organize your ideas for your paragraph. This graphic organizer has three parts: a beginning, middle, and end (conclusion). These sections refer to the different parts of the anecdote.

<table>
<tr><th></th><th>Who</th><th>What</th><th>When</th><th>Where</th><th colspan="2">Why</th></tr>
<tr><td>B
E
G
I
N
N
I
N
G</td><td></td><td></td><td></td><td></td><td colspan="2"></td></tr>
<tr><th></th><th colspan="2">Event 1</th><th colspan="2">Event 2</th><th colspan="2">Event 3</th></tr>
<tr><td>M
I
D
D
L
E</td><td colspan="2"></td><td colspan="2"></td><td colspan="2"></td></tr>
<tr><th></th><th colspan="2">Resolution</th><th colspan="4">Lesson</th></tr>
<tr><td>E
N
D</td><td colspan="2"></td><td colspan="4"></td></tr>
</table>

6 **Using a Graphic Organizer** Read the paragraphs that follow. Then fill in the graphic organizer above with information from the paragraphs.

One summer weekend, some friends and I decided to walk to a waterfall we had heard about. Since it was too far to walk along the road, we followed a railroad line. We had walked five or six miles when we came to a high rock wall where the tracks entered a tunnel. This tunnel didn't look very long, but it was very narrow. We knew it would be dangerous if a train came because there would be no safe place for us to go. However, we couldn't climb the rocks or walk around them, and no one wanted to go back. Finally, we decided to go through the tunnel. I knew it was foolish, but I went because the others did.

▲ Walking through train tunnels is extremely dangerous.

(continued on next page)

As soon as we entered the tunnel, we saw that it was longer and darker than we had thought. Suddenly everyone was frightened and we all began to run. "This is crazy!" I thought. As we ran faster, it got lighter in the tunnel. Once we were outside, we fell on the ground gasping. About a minute later, a train came through. That was when I finally realized the importance of thinking for myself.

Strategy

Using Two Paragraphs for an Anecdote

When writing an anecdote, you might need to begin a second paragraph for several different reasons. Here are some of them:

1. The time or place of the story changes.
2. You begin to describe a new person or event.
3. Something important happens in the story.
4. You stop telling the story and explain something about it.

7 Analyzing a Paragraph Change In the anecdote about the tunnel, what was the writer's reason for starting a new paragraph when he wrote, "As soon as we entered the tunnel . . ."?

Strategy

Using Details

Your anecdote will be more interesting if you can make the reader "live" the experience with you. One way to do this is by using sensory details to help the reader see and feel what you saw and felt. The more the reader *feels* the events of the story, the better he or she will understand the lesson the anecdote conveys.

8 Identifying Omissions Below is the second paragraph of the tunnel anecdote without some of the details. What details did the writer leave out? What effect do the omissions have on the anecdote?

We started to walk through the tunnel, but then we got frightened and started to run. After we got outside, a train came through. That was when I finally realized the importance of thinking for myself.

Strategy

Identifying Digressions
One difficulty with details is that they can easily become digressions. To *digress* means to go off of the topic. In a good anecdote, everything leads to the conclusion or lesson. If a detail leads *away* from the lesson (even if it is true and interesting), you should take it out of your anecdote. It is a digression.

9 Identifying Digressions Identify the two digressions in the following paragraph:

One summer weekend, some friends and I decided to walk to a waterfall we had heard about. This waterfall was called Horsetail Falls because it looked like a horse's tail. Many of the lakes and mountains were named for things that they looked like. There was also Camel's Hump Mountain and Elephant Ear Lake. There was a place to swim at the bottom, and it was a wonderful place for a picnic. We had never been there because it was on the other side of the mountain. It was several miles by road, and none us could drive yet. All of our parents worked, and there was no bus service. However, we knew that it was shorter if you didn't take the road and just walked over the mountain.

10 Evaluating a Writer's Decisions Below are the writer's notes for part of the tunnel anecdote on pages 89 and 90. In small groups, discuss the questions that follow.

didn't look very long	*a lot of bushes, more rocks*
narrow, dangerous	*on right*
rocks 80–100 ft. high	*couldn't go right or left*
couldn't climb them	*no trains all day—maybe tracks*
river on left	*unused?*

1. Which details did the writer leave out of the anecdote?
2. Do you agree with his or her decisions? Why or why not?

TOEFL® iBT

Focus on Testing

Personal Anecdotes on Writing Exams
In this chapter, you learned that personal anecdotes often teach a lesson or illustrate a point. When you're responding to independent writing prompts on the TOEFL® Internet-Based Test (iBT), you can use personal anecdotes as support for general statements.

Below is a sample independent writing prompt.

> *Should students have a role in deciding the rules at a school? For example, should a student government help make rules for the school (e.g., about dress codes or about class attendance)? State your opinion and support it with specific reasons and examples.*

To plan an answer to a prompt like this, think first about your experiences. Did your school allow some student government? Did student government help solve any problems? Did student government cause any problems? If you have no experience with student government, can you make up an anecdote that would fit here?

Make sure the anecdote you use supports your opinion. It should show either the good or the bad aspects of student government. If it does not illustrate the point you want to make, don't use it.

Practice Set a timer for 30 minutes. Plan and write your response to the prompt above. After you have finished, share your response with one or two other students in the class, and discuss each person's use of anecdotes as support.

Part 2 Developing Writing Skills

Developing Cohesion and Clarity

USING THE PAST PERFECT TENSE

In the anecdote about the tunnel, everything happened in the past. The writer mainly used the simple past tense to tell the story in the order that it happened. But the writer used the past perfect tense three times to show that one action happened before another one in the past.

The past perfect follows this structure: *had (not)* + past participle

Examples

We had been there many times.
She hadn't asked for permission to go.

When describing more than one event in the past, you can use the past perfect tense to show which action happened first.

Examples

I had already left by the time he got back.
(had ... left: first event; got back: second event)

We hadn't gone one mile when the car broke down.
(hadn't gone: first event; broke down: second event)

1 Identifying the Past Perfect Tense

Find the three sentences in the tunnel anecdote on pages 89 and 90 that include the past perfect tense. Write them in the chart below. Then write the event that happened earlier and later in each example.

In the Anecdote	Happened Earlier	Happened Later
1. *decided to walk to a waterfall we had heard about*		
2.		
3.		

2 Completing Sentences with the Correct Verb Form

The following passage is an early draft of the tunnel anecdote. You will notice that it still contains several digressions. Fill in the blanks with the simple past tense or the past perfect tense of the verbs in parentheses.

One summer weekend, some friends and I decided to take a picnic to a waterfall we had heard about. Some people ____________ (1) (drive) cars and ____________ (2) (take) the food, but the rest of us ____________ (3) (want) to walk. Since it was too far to walk along the road, we followed a railroad line. We had walked five or six miles when we came to a high rock wall where the tracks entered a tunnel. We ____________ (4) (be) surprised. Nobody ____________ (5) (tell) us about it. The tunnel didn't look very long, but it was narrow. We knew it would be dangerous if a train came. However, we couldn't climb the rocks or go around them, and no one wanted to go back. I ____________ (6) (have) a good breakfast, but some of the others ____________ (7) (not eat). They ____________ (8) (want) to get to the waterfall and have lunch. Finally we decided to go through. I knew it was foolish, but I went because the others did.

As soon as we entered the tunnel, we saw that it was longer and darker than we had thought. Earlier we ________________ (decide) to walk and
9
to stay together, but suddenly everyone was frightened and we all began to run. "This is crazy," I thought. "Why didn't I go back?" As we ran faster, it got lighter in the tunnel. Once we were outside, we fell on the ground gasping. No one ________________(fall) in the tunnel. We________________
10 11
(be) all safe. About a minute later, a train came through. We
________________(be) upset because we ________________(come)
12 13
so close to death. We ________________(be) also angry with ourselves
14
for being so foolish. Later we ________________(hear) that two boys
15
________________(die) in that tunnel before. That was when I finally re-
16
alized the importance of thinking for myself.

3 **Getting Rid of Digressions** Reread the preceding paragraph and decide which sentences are digressions and should be omitted. Cross them out.

4 **Writing the First Draft** Now you are ready to write your own anecdote. Use the experience you wrote about earlier, or choose another experience. Be sure to choose one that taught you a clear lesson.

Part 3 Revising and Editing

Revising for Content and Editing for Form

1 **Revising for Content** The following paragraph is the first part of an anecdote. The last sentence of the anecdote will be, "That was when I learned the satisfaction of doing hard work well." Cross out the digressions and irrelevant details.

▲ I didn't want to go to the farm. I wanted to hang out with my friends in the city.

The year I turned 15, my parents sent me to work on my uncle's farm for the summer. It was in South Carolina, and they had peach trees, cows, and chickens. They didn't make much money, and my father was always telling my uncle to sell the farm and come to Chicago. I didn't want to go to the farm, and I didn't like it when I got there. It was very hot and muggy most of the time. My cousins got up at 4:30 in the morning and went to bed at 9:00 at night, and in between, they worked. I had never worked on a farm before, so my cousin Wayne had to teach me everything, like milking the cows, driving the tractor, and so on. We were the same age, but I was bigger than he was. I was already six feet tall. Even so, I couldn't do anything as well as he could. I had a lot of friends at home, and we always hung around together, especially in the summer. I used to think about them. "They don't have to work on some dumb farm," I thought. "Why do I have to?"

2 Comparing Your Revisions Compare your revision to your classmates' work. Did you take out the same things?

3 Editing for Form The following paragraphs are a continuation of the anecdote above. Correct the underlined verbs if they are wrong.

I'm there about two weeks when Wayne and I have to load some bales of hay. After half an hour, we loaded a lot of bales and it was getting hard to throw them up onto the wagon. "I'm going to miss the next one," I thought. But Wayne missed first. His bale didn't go high enough and it has fallen back down. I took a deep breath and throw mine. I did it! "Hey Dad!"

(continued on next page)

Wayne called, "Did you see that?" I did it again and they cheer. I felt wonderful. After that everything change.

Wayne and I were friends and we enjoy competing with each other in everything. Usually he was better, but sometimes I am. I worked hard all summer and I love it. I learn a lot that summer, but the most important lesson is that day in the hayfield. That was when I learn the satisfaction of doing hard work well.

▲ When I got the hang of farm work, I actually started to have fun.

Evaluating Your Writing

4 Using a Rubric Read the rubric below with your class. Then use the rubric to score your paragraphs.

Score	Description
3 **Excellent**	▪ **Content:** Paragraphs present a story that leads to a lesson with sufficient information to keep the reader's interest and includes no unimportant details or digressions. ▪ **Organization:** Second paragraph starts in a place that makes sense. Sentences follow chronological order, and concluding sentence includes a lesson. ▪ **Vocabulary:** Vocabulary is varied, specific, and used correctly throughout. ▪ **Grammar:** Simple past, present perfect, and past perfect verb tenses are used correctly. ▪ **Spelling and Mechanics:** Words are spelled correctly throughout, and punctuation is correct.

2 **Adequate**	▪ **Content:** Paragraphs present a story that leads to a lesson. There may be some unimportant details or digressions. ▪ **Organization:** Sentences may follow chronological order. Paragraph division may not be clear. Lesson may not be in concluding sentence. ▪ **Vocabulary:** Vocabulary is mostly varied and specific and is used mostly correctly throughout. ▪ **Grammar:** Most simple past, present perfect, and past perfect verb tenses are used correctly. ▪ **Spelling and Mechanics:** Most words are spelled correctly, and punctuation is correct.
1 **Developing**	▪ **Content:** Writing does not present a story or a lesson. ▪ **Organization:** Sentences do not seem to follow chronological order; writing may not follow paragraph format. ▪ **Vocabulary:** Vocabulary is very limited, or there are too many mistakes to understand the ideas. ▪ **Grammar:** Many grammar mistakes make the writing confusing to the reader. ▪ **Spelling and Mechanics:** There are many distracting spelling and punctuation mistakes.

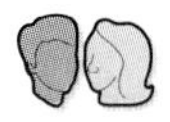

5 Peer Sharing Read another classmate's anecdote. Do you understand the order of events? Is there any part that needs more explanation? Do you understand the lesson?

6 Writing the Second Draft Rewrite your anecdote using your rubric evaluation. Revise for content, and edit for form. Then give your anecdote to your teacher for comments. When your teacher returns your paper, ask him or her about any comments you don't understand.

Part 4 Expansion Activities

1 Sharing Your Writing Read two of your classmates' anecdotes. Then answer these questions about each anecdote:

1. What exactly made the anecdote interesting for you? Be specific. You can mention the incidents, some of the details, the lesson, or something else.
2. Do you agree with the student's conclusion (lesson) or not? Briefly explain why or why not.

2 Writing a Narrative Write down the story you wrote about in Activity 3 on page 87, or write another story that teaches a lesson or has a moral. Be sure to include the moral of the story at the end. Then follow these steps:

- Form small groups, and read each other's stories.
- Discuss the similarities in the stories if there are any.
- Discuss which story is the most interesting and why.
- Collect all the stories and make copies for your classmates to read.

3 Writing in Your Journal Spend 20 minutes free writing in your journal. Choose one of the following topics:

1. An anecdote about a frustrating day or experience you had
2. An anecdote about something funny that happened to you
3. An anecdote about a frightening experience

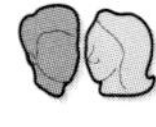

4 Researching Fables Every country has fables, fictional stories that teach lessons. Some of the most famous Greek fables are Aesop's. Research a fable by Aesop online. Follow these steps:

1. Use the following combination of words in a search engine:

    fables + morals + Aesop

2. Choose one of the fables that you find. Read it and answer these questions:
    - What is the lesson or moral of this fable?
    - Does your native country have a similar fable?

3. Retell the fable to a classmate. Have him or her guess what the lesson is.

▲ Aesop's fables are popular among children.

Self-Assessment Log

In this chapter, you worked through the activities listed below. How much did they help you to become a better writer? Check *A lot*, *A little*, or *Not at all*.

	A lot	**A little**	**Not at all**
I identified and discussed the moral of a story.	❑	❑	❑
I used a graphic organizer to plan a narrative.	❑	❑	❑
I learned when to start a new paragraph in a narrative.	❑	❑	❑
I practiced using details to enhance the reader's experience.	❑	❑	❑
I practiced using the past perfect tense.	❑	❑	❑
I learned to identify and omit digressions.	❑	❑	❑
I used a writing rubric to evaluate my first draft.	❑	❑	❑
(Add something) ________________________________	❑	❑	❑

____

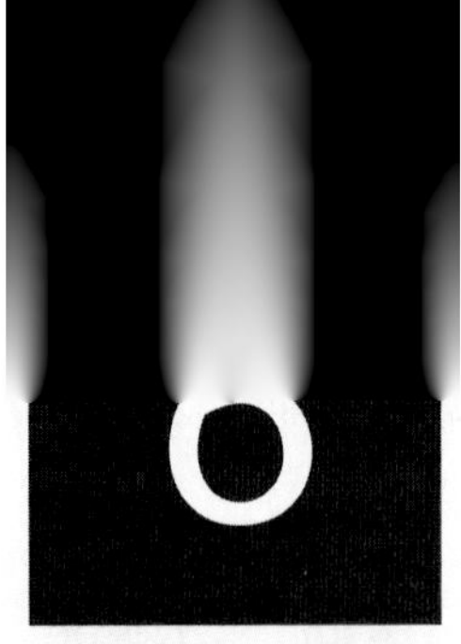

Global Connections

In This Chapter

Genre Focus: Argument

Writing Product

Two argument paragraphs for or against globalization

Writing Process

- Use examples to define a broad term.
- Use a clustergram to organize information for an argument.
- Write a topic sentence for argument paragraphs.
- Use the correct form of a word.
- Use and punctuate relative clauses.
- Use specific examples to support an argument.
- Evaluate Internet sources.

“To travel is to discover that everyone is wrong about other countries.”

—Aldous Huxley
English novelist (1894–1963)

Connecting to the Topic

1. Do you communicate with people who live far away? How do you do it?
2. What connections do people in your town or city have with other countries?
3. What are some examples of international businesses in your community?

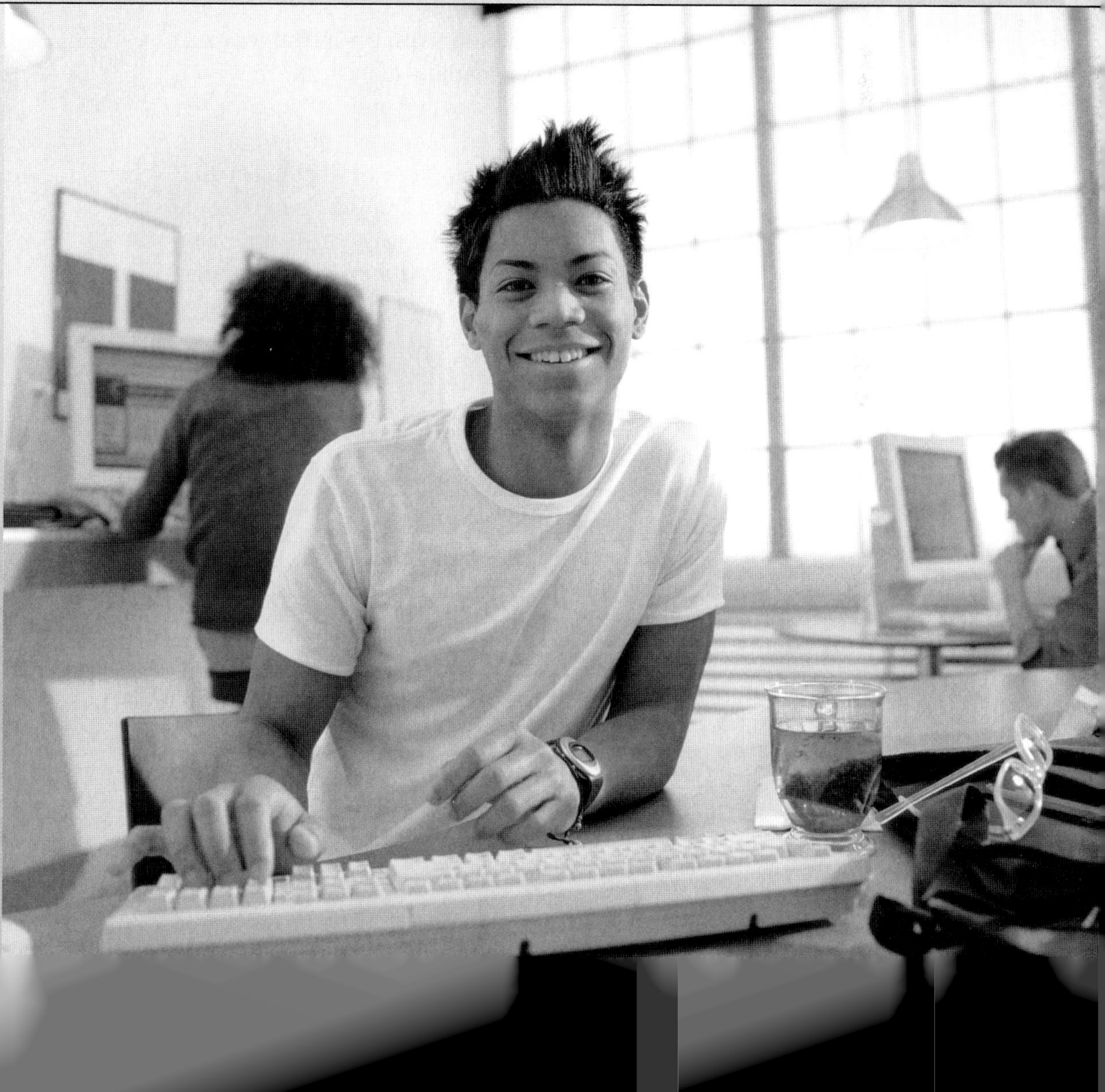

Part 1 Before You Write

Exploring Ideas

Marshall McLuhan

Marshall McLuhan (1911–1980) was a Canadian professor and writer interested in modern communications. In his 1967 book *Understanding Media*, McLuhan wrote that "the new electronic interdependence recreates the world in the image of the global village." At that time, McLuhan was referring to how television allowed people all over the world to share information. With the introduction of technologies such as satellite dishes, the Internet, and email, we have moved beyond the idea of the global village to a process many call *globalization*, the movement toward markets and policies that go beyond national borders. Due to technological advances, specifically rapid forms of communication, travel, and e-commerce, the events of one part of the world have a significant impact on the rest of the world.

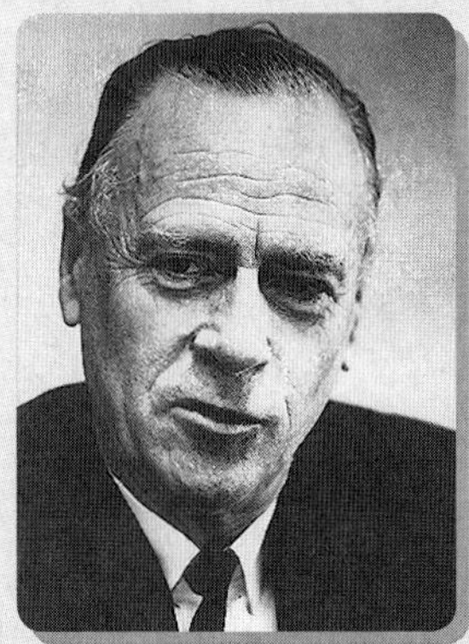

▲ Marshall McLuhan

Strategy

Expanding a Definition

In this chapter, you are going to write two paragraphs that argue for globalization and its benefits or against globalization and its negative effects. There are many different aspects of globalization: communication, travel, business, health, culture, and environment. Within each of these topics, there are many positive and negative issues related to globalization. To write a good argument for or against globalization, you will first need to choose one aspect of the term and define it.

1 Defining a Term With a group of three students, discuss the photos below. Discuss the ways in which they illustrate globalization. Then discuss what globalization means to each person in your group. How has it affected each person's life?

▲ The impact of globalization can be seen in many different ways.

Building Vocabulary

2 Using a Vocabulary Chart Below are some words that are often used in the context of globalization. Work with two other students, and discuss these words. Look up any words you don't know. Complete the chart by adding words that you used in your discussion in Activity 1.

Nouns	Verbs	Adjectives
diversity	export	diverse
e-commerce	globalize	global
globe	import	multicultural
immigrant	influence	multinational
market		technological
multiculturalism		transnational
resources		
technology		
telecommunications		

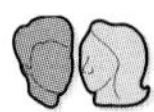

3 Using New Vocabulary Work with a partner. Discuss the following questions:

1. How does immigration increase diversity?
2. Is a multicultural society diverse? Why or why not?
3. How does technology affect telecommunications?
4. How is e-commerce different from traditional commerce?
5. What is better for a country—imports or exports? Why?
6. How are multinational and transnational companies different?

4 Analyzing Prefixes and Suffixes Look at the words below. How did the suffixes and prefixes change their part of speech? If necessary, use a dictionary to help you.

1. multiculturalism

Root	Prefix/Suffix	New Word	Change
culture	+ al =	*cultural*	*noun to adjective*
culture	+ multi + al =	______	______
culture	+ multi + al + ism =	______	______

2. immigration

Root	Prefix/Suffix	New Word	Change
migrate	+ tion =	______	______
migrate	+ im + tion =	______	______

3. telecommunication

Root	Prefix/Suffix	New Word	Change
communicate	+ tion =	______	______
communicate	+ tele + tion =	______	______

4. transnational

Root	Prefix/Suffix	New Word	Change
nation	+ al =	______	______
nation	+ trans + al =	______	______

5. globalization

Root	Prefix/Suffix	New Word	Change
globe	+ al =	______	______
globe	+ al + ize	______	______
globe	+al +ize + ation	______	______

6. technological

Root	Prefix/Suffix	New Word	Change
technology	+ ical	______	______

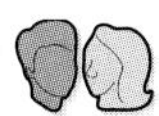

What Do You Think?

Defining Broad Terms

The many different interpretations of the term *globalization* illustrate the importance of defining certain terms when you write about them. You can define a term by saying what it means to you or by describing how you are using it in a particular context. The best way to illustrate exactly what you mean by a particular word is to provide a concrete example of it.

Using Examples to Define Broad Terms

With a partner, define the following words by giving examples of each of them.

diversity	globalization	interdependence	multiculturalism

Organizing Ideas

5 Listing Information In groups of three, discuss the good and bad effects of globalization. Fill in the following chart with notes from your discussion

Good Effects	Bad Effects
multiculturalism	*more social inequalities*

6 Choosing a Side Look over your notes, and add any other ideas you have about the effects of globalization. Then decide if you would like to argue in favor of or against globalization.

Using Graphic Organizers

Strategy

Using Clustergrams
A clustergram is a graphic organizer that you can use to generate and organize ideas. It can help you decide which ideas to focus on when a topic is very broad. In a clustergram, the topic is in the center, and related ideas are connected to each other around it. Once you've filled in your clustergram, you'll be able to see which of the arguments are strong and which aren't. Then you can decide which ones to use in your paragraphs.

Globalization

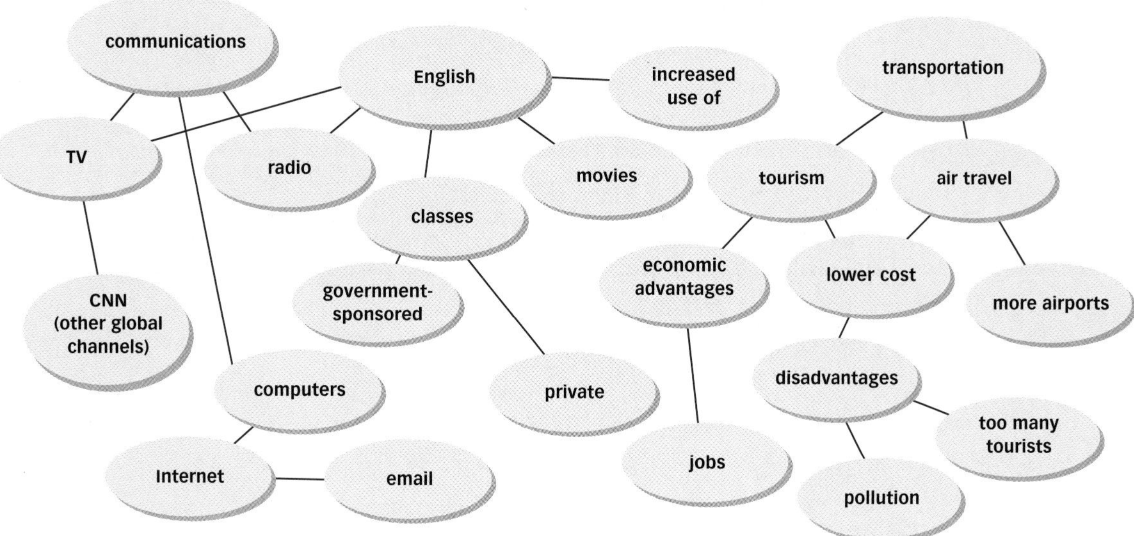

7 Analyzing a Graphic Organizer Look at the clustergram above with a partner, and answer the following questions:

1. What is the topic? Is the author for or against the idea explored here?
2. What are the main ideas related to the topic?
3. Can you add details to the ideas that currently don't have any?

8 Creating a Graphic Organizer Create a clustergram. First, write down all your ideas either for or against globalization. Then circle them and connect ideas that are related.

9 Choosing Your Arguments Look at your clustergram and decide which ideas you want to use for your paragraphs. You should choose three arguments in favor of globalization or against it. You will need one or two examples for each argument. Write notes for them below.

Arguments	Examples

Strategy

Writing a Topic Sentence

The topic sentence of a two-paragraph argument should state the main idea of both paragraphs. It should also contain your opinion on the topic.

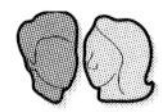

10 Choosing the Best Topic Sentence With a partner, read the sentences below. Then discuss which one you think is a good topic sentence and why.

1. One aspect of globalization is the expansion of trade and policies beyond national borders.
2. Can globalization be stopped?
3. Although many people are against globalization, it has many benefits for people in poorer countries.
4. Globalization is bad.
5. Globalization causes many more problems than it solves.

▲ The effects of globalization are felt among the wealthy as well as the poor.

Part 2 Developing Writing Skills

Developing Cohesion and Clarity

Strategy

Using the Correct Form of a Word

Many words have different forms for different parts of speech. When you write, be careful to use the correct forms of words.

Examples

I have an appointment for a medical <u>examination</u> today.

The doctor <u>examined</u> the young boy.

The medical <u>examiner</u> said that the man had died from a heart attack.

1 Completing Sentences with the Correct Form of a Word

Complete each sentence below with the correct form of the word in parentheses.

1. Many countries are worried about increasing _immigration_ (immigrate) and have strict laws to control the number of people who can become citizens.
2. ________________ (tourist) is an important source of revenue for a lot of countries.
3. Many cities in the United States have a ________________ (multiculturalism) atmosphere. This can easily be seen in their great ________________ (diverse) of ethnic restaurants.
4. The world is truly becoming ________________ (interdependence). No country today can survive in ________________ (isolate).
5. It is almost impossible to keep up with all the recent ________________ (technology) changes.

USING RELATIVE CLAUSES

The relative pronouns *who*, *which*, *where*, and *that* can be used to introduce relative clauses, also called *adjective clauses*. A relative clause answers the question *Who*? or *Which one*?

The relative clauses are underlined in the following examples:

Examples

The woman who/that runs the restaurant is Japanese.	*Who* refers to people. *That* refers to people and things
The watch that/which I bought you is Swiss.	*Which* refers to things. *That* refers to people and things.
The office where I work employs people from four different countries.	*Where* refers to places.

---

2 Completing Sentences with Relative Pronouns

Complete the following sentences with the correct relative pronouns.

1. Globalization is inevitable, and people _who_ do not realize this are going to be left behind.
2. Transnational companies ________________ pay fair wages are welcome everywhere.
3. The global village is a place ________________ many languages are spoken; however, the one ________________ is predominant is English.
4. The car parts ________________ I just bought were made in six different countries.
5. Some futurists foresee the world as city-states ________________ are connected by technology.

Strategy

Supporting an Argument with Examples
Your argument will be stronger if you use one or two specific examples to support each of your statements.

Example
One problem with globalization is the destruction of the environment. For example, many transnational companies have factories near the border of the United States and Mexico. These companies do not have to follow U.S. laws, so they pollute the air and water in Mexico.

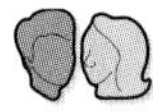

3 Choosing the Best Argument Read the two paragraphs below. Then work with a partner and discuss which one is more persuasive and why.

1 One of the most beneficial aspects of globalization is the movement of people across borders. For example, in the small town where I live in Mexico, there are now shops owned and operated by people from China. For people in town, the Chinese are not quite as "foreign" as they were before. There are many other examples as well. Last year when I traveled to Dublin, I met a Spanish waitress, a Polish store clerk, a Romanian bus driver, and a Tahitian chef. Cities and towns across the world are starting to resemble the United Nations.

▲ Because of globalization, many different countries do business together.

2 One of the most beneficial aspects of globalization is the movement of people across borders. Lots of people are moving to work in other countries. They are studying foreign languages and learning to get along with people from other cultures. This is good because the more people work and live together, the better they understand each other.

4 Adding Supporting Examples Look at your clustergram and the notes you made for your paragraph. Do you need to add more examples to support your arguments?

5 Writing the First Draft Write your argument paragraphs. Be sure to include your opinion on globalization in the topic sentence and to define what aspect of globalization you are writing about.

Part 3 Revising and Editing

Revising for Content and Editing for Form

1 Revising for Content Read the following paragraph. Then rewrite it combining sentences with relative clauses where needed. Then add a concluding sentence to the paragraph.

Some people think that learning a foreign language is a waste of time. This is not true. People study foreign languages. These people learn more about other cultures. Other people are monolingual. They understand very little about other countries. Of course some people study dead languages like Latin. You can't really learn about other places by studying a language that no one speaks.

PUNCTUATING RELATIVE CLAUSES

There are two different types of relative clauses: restrictive and nonrestrictive.

Restrictive Relative Clauses

A restrictive relative clause tells you which person, place, or thing the writer is referring to. The information in the restrictive relative clause is necessary to complete the sentence. Don't use commas with restrictive clauses.

Examples

Children <u>who are bilingual</u> have an advantage over their monolingual playmates.
May and October are the months <u>that I like best</u>.

Note that if you omit the restrictive relative clauses *who are bilingual* (example 1) and *that I like best* (example 2), the thoughts are incomplete.

Nonrestrictive Relative Clauses

A nonrestrictive relative clause gives additional information. This additional information is not necessary to complete the idea in the sentence. In nonrestrictive clauses, use *which* instead of *that* to refer to things, and use *who* instead of *that* to refer to people. Use commas to separate a nonrestrictive clause from the rest of the sentence.

Examples

May and October, <u>which have the best weather</u>, are my favorite months.
My brother's children, <u>who are bilingual</u>, are seven and ten years old.

Note that if you omit the nonrestrictive relative clauses *who are bilingual* (example 1) and *which have the best weather* (example 2), the sentences are still complete.

---

2 Editing for Form Read the sentences, and add commas where necessary.

1. The global village, which was first discussed by Marshall McLuhan in the 1960s, has finally come to be.
2. The teachers who teach in the global village should have a multicultural point of view.
3. My father works in a cement factory that is owned by Japanese businessmen.
4. New technology which is the backbone of globalization is growing at a faster rate than ever.
5. Transnational companies that operate in the third world often do great damage to the environment.
6. World markets are controlled by huge corporations that may not care about their workers.

Evaluating Your Writing

3 Using a Rubric Read the rubric below with your class. Then use the rubric to score your paragraphs.

Score	Description
3 **Excellent**	■ **Content:** Paragraphs present an opinion about globalization and explain and defend writer's arguments by using specific examples. ■ **Organization:** Paragraphs are introduced by a topic sentence, and all sentences connect to this main idea. Writer's opinion is stated in the topic sentence. Examples are grouped with related arguments. ■ **Vocabulary:** Vocabulary is specific, varied, and used correctly throughout. ■ **Grammar:** Relative clauses are used correctly, and correct forms of words are used throughout. ■ **Spelling and Mechanics:** Words are spelled correctly, and capitalization and punctuation are correct.

WRITING WITH COMPUTERS

The Internet is a valuable source of information, particularly about current events. However, you must be careful when quoting from an Internet source. Only use information that comes from a legitimate source such as a major news organization or a well-known university or other group. In addition, try to find the same information from at least three other reliable sites.

2 **Adequate**	■ **Content:** Paragraphs present a point of view about globalization, but writer's arguments may not be fully supported by examples. ■ **Organization:** Paragraphs have a topic sentence, but some ideas may not be relevant. Some examples may not be grouped with related arguments. ■ **Vocabulary:** Vocabulary is specific and varied, but a few words may be used incorrectly. ■ **Grammar:** Some relative clauses are used correctly. Correct forms of words are used throughout. ■ **Spelling and Mechanics:** Most words are spelled correctly, and capitalization and punctuation are correct.
1 **Developing**	■ **Content:** Paragraphs do not present the writer's opinion on globalization or do not include examples to support arguments. ■ **Organization:** Paragraphs do not contain a topic sentence, or several ideas do not connect to the topic sentence. Examples are not grouped with related arguments. ■ **Vocabulary:** Vocabulary is limited, and there are too many mistakes to understand or follow the ideas. ■ **Grammar:** Relative clauses are not used correctly or are not used at all. Incorrect forms of words are used. ■ **Spelling and Mechanics:** Paragraphs include many distracting spelling and punctuation mistakes.

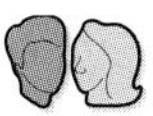

4 Peer Sharing Exchange papers with a classmate who disagrees with your views on globalization. Is his or her argument persuasive? Why or why not? Discuss your answers with your partner.

5 Writing the Second Draft Rewrite your paragraphs using your rubric evaluation. Revise for content, and edit for form. Then give your paper to your teacher for comments. When your paper is returned, ask your teacher about any comments you don't understand.

TOEFL® IBT

Focus on Testing

Using Graphic Organizers

In this chapter, you practiced clustering. Clustergrams and other kinds of graphic organizers can help you save time when you are writing under pressure. Take a few minutes before you start writing in a testing situation to use a graphic organizer to brainstorm ideas, see how they are connected, and choose the ideas that you want to focus on.

Practice Imagine you are asked to write about the positive or negative impact of the rising use of cars in cities. Take 5 minutes to draw a graphic organizer that includes your thoughts on this topic. Then share your work with a classmate and discuss your organizers.

Part 4 Expansion Activities

1 Researching Globalization Find an article about globalization in a newspaper or on the Internet. Does the writer mention any effects that you and your classmates have not thought of? If so, write them down and share them with the class.

2 Doing Research in Your Community Do research on the local effects of globalization. Work in groups. Go to local shops and find out the following information:

1. Where are the shop owners from?
2. What types of items are imported—clothing, food, electrical appliances?
3. Are there any transnational corporations in your town?

3 Interviewing Someone About Globalization Interview an older friend or relative about how his or her world has changed in the past 30 to 40 years. Take notes. Then, in small groups, share your findings with other classmates.

TIME CAPSULES

A time capsule is an encased collection of items that can tell people in the future something about the way people lived when the capsule was made. Some people put such items in a box or other container, close the container, and put it away or bury it. They write instructions telling people not to open it for 100 years or more.

4 Creating a Time Capsule Work in small groups. Brainstorm a list of items to put in a time capsule. Then choose only ten items for your capsule. When you finish, join another group, and share your lists. How are your items similar? How are they different? Why did you choose these items?

5 Writing in Your Journal Write about one of the following topics for 15 minutes:

1. How you think your world will change in the next 20 years
2. An aspect of globalization that interests you

6 Researching Opposing Arguments Search for websites with information about globalization. Find an article that you agree with and one that you do not agree with. Choose one and write a paragraph about why you agree or disagree. You can use the following words in your search:

globalization + positive effects or benefits

globalization + negative effects or problems

Self-Assessment Log

In this chapter, you worked through the activities listed below. How much did they help you to become a better writer? Check *A lot, A little,* or *Not at all.*

	A lot	A little	Not at all
I learned about using specific examples to define a broad term.	❑	❑	❑
I learned to use a clustergram to organize ideas.	❑	❑	❑
I learned to write a topic sentence for two argument paragraphs.	❑	❑	❑
I learned to choose the correct part of speech.	❑	❑	❑
I learned to use and punctuate relative clauses.	❑	❑	❑
I practiced using specific examples to support an argument.	❑	❑	❑
I used a writing rubric to evaluate my first draft.	❑	❑	❑
I learned tips for evaluating Internet resources.	❑	❑	❑
(Add something) ________________________________	❑	❑	❑

____

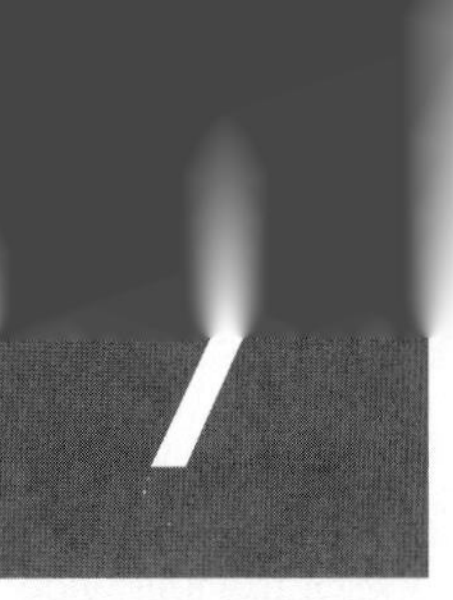

Language and Communication

In This Chapter

Genre Focus: Narrative

Writing Product

A narrative essay about a classmate

Writing Process

- Interview a classmate about living abroad.
- Use *-ed* and *-ing* adjectives to describe feelings.
- Learn to focus on one subject.
- Learn to organize information in a three paragraph essay.
- Learn to write introductions and conclusions.
- Use gerund subjects.
- Identify and correct parallelism problems.
- Use *would* and *used to* to talk about the past.

"Everywhere immigrants have enriched and strengthened the fabric of American life."

—John F. Kennedy
United States president (1917–1963)

Connecting to the Topic

1. Do you know anyone who has lived in a foreign county?
2. What kinds of problems did they face?
3. Would you live in another country if you had the chance? Why or why not?

Part 1 Before You Write

Exploring Ideas

1 Discussing Why People Live Abroad In small groups, discuss the various reasons people move to another country. List the reasons on the following lines.

Learn a new language

____

____

____

____

____

____

____

____

____

▲ Many people choose to live and study in foreign countries.

2 Discussing Difficulties Living Abroad With a partner, discuss some of the problems that newcomers to your native country might have. List them on the following lines:

Finding affordable housing

____

____

____

____

____

____

____

____

____

Strategy

Brainstorming Questions Before an Interview

In this chapter, you are going to write a narrative essay about a classmate's experience living in a foreign country. Before you write, you'll interview your classmate. It's a good idea to brainstorm and list interview questions before you conduct an interview.

3 Listing Interview Questions Make a list of questions to ask a classmate about his or her experience living in a foreign country where she or he did not speak the native language.

What Do You Think?

Distinguishing Appropriate and Inappropriate Questions

A narrative is a story. For your narrative essay, you will be interviewing someone to get information for a story. When you do this, it's important to know which questions are appropriate or polite to ask and which are not. The appropriateness of a question will depend on the person's cultural background, your familiarity with the person, and the purpose or topic of the interview.

Evaluating Questions

Work with a partner, and read the following list of questions. Discuss whether each question would be appropriate to ask. Write *yes* next to the appropraté questions and *no* next to the inappropriate ones.

1. *no* How old are you?
2. _______ When did you leave your country?
3. _______ Why don't you speak the native language well?
4. _______ What do you do for a living?
5. _______ Why aren't you married?
6. _______ What religion are you?
7. _______ How much money do you make?
8. _______ Where did/do you go to school?
9. _______ What do you think of the government of the country you moved to?
10. _______ What's your favorite food?
11. _______ Do you have children? If not, why not?

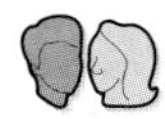

4 Interviewing a Classmate Work with a partner. Take turns interviewing each other. Answer the questions as yourself, or pretend to be someone else and make up answers. Take notes on your partner's answers.

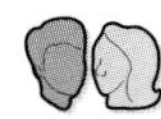

5 Adding to Your Interviewers' Notes Exchange notes. What else can you add to the notes your partner wrote?

Building Vocabulary

6 Using a Vocabulary Chart In your discussions, you may have heard some unfamiliar words, or you may not know the word for some of the ideas you wanted to express. Look up those words and add them to the following chart containing words used to discuss the immigrant experience.

Nouns	Verbs	Adjectives
confusion	confuse	anxious
depression	depress	confused
excitement	emigrate	depressed
homeland	excite	excited
humiliation	humiliate	homesick
native land	immigrate	humiliated
refugee	thrill	thrilled
thrill		upset
		frightened
		disappointed
		surprised

7 Identifying Specific Adjectives Look at the adjectives listed in Activity 6. Which ones describe pleasant feelings? Which ones describe unpleasant feelings? Write them in the correct column in the chart on the next page.

Pleasant Feelings	Unpleasant Feelings
excitement	

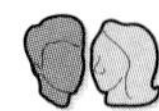

8 Using New Vocabulary Work with a partner. Answer the following questions related to the new vocabulary words.

1. What confuses you?
2. Would you feel humiliated in any of these situations? Why or why not?
   - You give a wrong answer in class.
   - You drop a tray full of food in the cafeteria.
   - You forget to take a book back to the library.
3. Have you ever been depressed? Why?
4. Which of these words is a synonym for *anxious*?

   shy *worried* *happy* *quiet*
5. What kinds of experiences upset you?

USING *-ED* AND *-ING* ADJECTIVES TO DESCRIBE FEELINGS

Many *-ed* and *-ing* adjectives describe emotions. Adjectives ending in *-ed* often describe the person, animal, or thing that *has* the feeling, whereas *-ing* adjectives often describe the person, animal, or thing that *creates* the feeling.

Examples

Eva heard some surprising news. (The news created the feeling of surprise.)
She was surprised by the news. (She *has a feeling* of surprise.)

Below is a list of some common *-ed* and *-ing* adjectives.

confused	confusing	humiliated	humiliating
depressed	depressing	surprised	surprising
disappointed	disappointing	tired	tiring
excited	exciting	terrified	terrifying
frightened	frightening	thrilled	thrilling

9 **Identifying Cause and Effect** Look at the sentences below. Circle the phrase that the *-ed* or *-ing* adjective describes.

1. At first, (not being able to understand the language) was terrifying to Ahmad.
2. Tran was disappointed when he couldn't find a job.
3. Living in a new country is confusing to most people.
4. Wilma was surprised that learning English was so easy.
5. Daoud was thrilled at winning the French prize.

10 **Completing Sentences with *-ed* and *-ing* Adjectives** Complete the sentences below with the adjective form of the words in the box.

depress	frighten	tire	excite	surprise

1. Tran was *surprised* ________ by British customs.
2. Amara thought working full time and studying was ________________ .
3. Alain was ________________ and homesick when he first moved to Germany.
4. At first, Junko thought that life in New York was ________________ , but later she got very lonely.
5. Some people think that flying is ________________ .

11 **Completing Sentences with *-ed* and *-ing* Adjectives** Complete each sentence below with an *-ed* or *-ing* adjective.

1. Life in a foreign country can be *thrilling* ________ .
2. I was ________________ on the first day of class.
3. Leaving home is ________________ .
4. My friends and family were ________________ when I left.
5. When it was time to go back to my home country, I was ________________ .
6. The next time I live in a foreign country, I won't be as ________________ .

12 **Writing Sentences with *-ed* and *-ing* Adjectives** Use *-ed* and *-ing* adjectives to write three sentences about the topic of your narrative essay.

Strategy

Organizing Ideas

Organizing a Narrative Essay

Your narrative essay will have three paragraphs. Following is an outline of what each paragraph should include.

First paragraph (introduction)
Background information about the person
Information about why the person left his or her native country

Second paragraph (Body Paragraph)
Main events of the story told in chronological order
Answers to the questions:

- What happened when the person arrived in the new country?
- How did he or she feel?
- What happened next?
- How did that change the way he or she felt?

Third paragraph (Conclusion)
Resolution of the story
Look to the future

Using Graphic Organizers

13 **Using Graphic Organizers** Use the organizer below to arrange the information that will go in the body of your narrative essay. Look at the notes from your interview, and list the events that your partner told you about in chronological order.

First event: ______________________________
____
____

Second event: ______________________________
____
____

Third event: ______________________________
____
____

Strategy

Staying Focused on the Subject

When you write, be careful to stay focused on the subject. All of the information that you give should be closely related to the topic of your essay. When you read the first draft of your essay, be sure to cross out all irrelevant information and digressions.

14 **Eliminating Irrelevant Information** Read the narrative essay below, and cross out any sentences that don't belong.

Ahn Kim never planned to study outside her native Korea. Her brother was a student in Massachusetts, but Ahn Kim was happy to stay in Seoul with her family. One day a letter came from Ahn's uncle. He needed help. He invited Ahn to go to work in his shop in New York City. Ahn's uncle sold fruit and vegetables in a small shop in Queens. Ahn's parents thought it was a good opportunity. Ahn didn't want to disappoint them, so she went.

▲ Ahn Kim left home to work in her uncle's store.

When Ahn Kim first arrived in the United States from Korea, she was very sad and frightened. She was living with her uncle's family in their small crowded apartment. She worked in the shop every day. She could speak to her aunt and uncle, but she couldn't communicate with anyone else. The world outside of the shop and the apartment was almost totally incomprehensible to her. Ahn could not read a street sign, ask a question, or understand directions. Ahn's brother spoke English well. He had lived in the United States for a long time. Ahn's life changed for the better when she decided to go to Newton Community College to take English classes. This school is located on the corner of Broad Street and First Avenue.

Today Ahn is still studying English. She has also enrolled in business classes at the community college. She moved out of her uncle's apartment and into a rooming house with other young people. She has many friends. Although she still plans on returning to Korea, she is happy and grateful that she had the chance to go to the United States.

Strategy

Writing Introductions

The introduction to your narrative essay should give background information about the person you interviewed. It should describe the person's life before he or she moved to a new country and explain the reason the person moved.

15 **Writing an Introduction** Write some ideas for information that will go into the first paragraph of your essay.

Strategy

Writing Conclusions

The conclusion to your narrative essay should be a resolution to the narrative. It can describe how the person solved the problem that he or she had or explain how the person's life today is different than it was. It could also include thoughts on what the future holds for your interviewee.

16 **Writing a Conclusion** Write some ideas for information that will go into the conclusion of your essay.

17 **Analyzing the Organization of an Essay** Read the narrative essay below. With a partner, discuss the following questions about the organization of the essay:

1. What information does the introduction provide? What questions does it answer?
2. What information does the body paragraph provide? Can you list the things that happened?
3. What information does the conclusion provide?

All of his life, Joel had dreamt about traveling to a foreign country. His parents didn't have enough money to pay for him to go abroad, so Joel studied hard and hoped that one day he would get an opportunity. One day, his school announced a competition for a scholarship to study in Canada. Joel entered the competition and won.

Joel was thrilled when he heard about winning the scholarship. He was going to study art in Canada. He didn't cry when he said good-bye to his family. He couldn't wait to get to Canada. He was excited about going to the university and meeting people from all over the world. However, after a few weeks away from his native country, Joel felt very unhappy. He was homesick and lonely. The other students were nice, but it was hard for him to speak English all day. His classes were interesting, but they were hard. He had to spend many hours every day working in the library. It was a lonely life. He began to wish he hadn't won the scholarship at all.

Then after two or three months, Joel began to feel better. His English improved, and he spent more time with other students. Now he is very happy. The university feels like home, and his friends feel like family. Joel still remembers how bad he felt at first, but now it seems like a lifetime ago to him.

18 **Reviewing Your Notes** Look at the notes you've written for your narrative essay. Is there any information that seems irrelevant? Is there any information you should add?

TOEFL® iBT

Focus on Testing

Developing Your Ideas

To get information for the essay in this chapter, you wrote questions and interviewed someone. You can also use questions when you write an essay on a timed test. However, in this case, the person you interview will be yourself. After you write, take a few minutes to ask yourself *wh-* questions (*who, what, where, when, how,* and *why*) about each sentence in your paragraph. If your essay already answers each question, congratulations! You probably have a well-developed essay. If not, add information to develop your ideas further.

Practice Read the following outline. Ask yourself *wh-* questions to find out what information is missing. Use your imagination to add details to each section. When you are finished, compare your outline with a classmate's. Did you both add the same types of information?

Introduction

Marsha Foster was very excited when her company offered her a job in a foreign country.

Body Paragraph

When she first arrived in the new country, her life was very difficult.

Conclusion

Then her life changed. Now she is very happy. She doesn't want to go back to her country.

Part 2 Developing Writing Skills

Developing Cohesion and Clarity

USING GERUND SUBJECTS

A gerund is the *-ing* form of a verb used as a noun—for example, *moving*, *becoming*, *working*. (See Appendix 1 for rules for spelling changes.) Gerunds or gerund phrases are sometimes subjects of sentences. These are called *gerund subjects*.

Examples
Moving to the United States was the most exciting experience of Juan's life.
Being sent to live in Paris made Joseph nervous.
Learning French was very difficult for Michael.

You can make a gerund subject negative by adding *not* before the gerund.

Examples
Not being able to read street signs was the hardest part of living in Turkey.
Not knowing any English made it difficult to find my way around the airport in London.

1 Writing Sentences with Gerund Subjects Write sentences by making a gerund subject from the words in parentheses.

1. (Work in a foreign country) is exciting but stressful.
   Working in a foreign country is exciting but stressful.
   ____

2. (Learn to live in a new culture) is difficult for anyone.
   ____
   ____

3. (Leave your homeland) is never easy.
   ____
   ____

4. ([Not] be able to even order lunch) was humiliating for Gloria.
   ____
   ____

5. ([Not] speak the language) made Jaime feel isolated.
   ____
   ____

2 Completing Sentences with Gerund Subjects

Complete the sentences below with a gerund subject.

1. *Having a conversation in a foreign language* for the first time is a thrilling experience.
2. ________________ made Marta very happy.
3. ________________ can be very tiring.
4. ________________ is important to Yoko.
5. ________________ was easy for Katrina.

USING GERUNDS AND INFINITIVES IN PARALLEL CONSTRUCTION

When you write, it is important to use gerunds and infinitives in parallel construction. That is, infinitives should be paired with infinitives, and gerunds should be paired with gerunds. The gerunds and infinitives in the following sentences are parallel. The sentences are correct.

Examples

Gerunds: <u>Working</u> during the day and <u>studying</u> at night made Miguel very tired.
Infinitives: I am too tired <u>to speak</u> English all day and <u>study</u> English all night.

Note that *to* in the infinitive *to study* is implied.

The gerunds and infinitives in the following sentences are not parallel. In both cases, a gerund is paired with an infinitive. The sentences are incorrect.

Examples

<u>Visiting</u> new places and <u>to meet</u> new people always interested Shadi.
<u>Going</u> to the movies and <u>to watch</u> television helped Henry improve his Japanese.

---

3 Identifying Parallelism Problems

The following paragraph includes some parallelism errors. Find the mistakes and correct them.

A Difficult Decision

Deciding ~~To decide to~~ leave her country and going to the United States was very difficult for Berta. Unfortunately, in her native country, she was unable to go to school or finding a good job. When her husband suggested that they leave, she knew he was right. However, when she first arrived in the United States,

▲ Leaving home was difficult for Berta.

she was very unhappy. Not being able to speak English well and not making friends made it difficult for her to feel at home. In addition, she and her husband hardly saw each other. To work during the day and going to school at night meant that there was little time for them to be together. That was five years ago. Now they both speak English and have good jobs. They also have a daughter and a son. Although leaving was not easy, Berta knows that she made the right decision. Leaving the unknown and to live in a totally new country is difficult.

USING *WOULD* AND *USED TO* TO TALK ABOUT THE PAST

When English speakers talk about past events, they often use the simple past tense. However, when they are talking about past habits or routines, they sometimes use *would* + verb or *used to* + verb.

Examples

When I was young, I would get up early every morning.
When I was young, I used to get up early every morning.

You can use *would* and *used to* to talk about repeated activities. However, you can't use *would* for nonaction verbs such as *have*, *think*, *live*, *believe*, and *own*.

Examples

Her grandfather used to have a long white beard.
She used to think that he was the oldest man in the world.

Remember that you cannot use *would* and *used to* for activities that happened only once or twice, or states and events that continued for only a short time. In these cases you must use the simple past tense.

Examples

Anna started school when she was seven.
On the first day of school, she was afraid because she thought that her mother was leaving her forever.

Instead of using *used to* too often in one paragraph, it's better to use *used to* as well as *would* or the simple past tense for variety.

---

4 Completing Sentences with the Past Tense, *Used To*, or *Would*

Complete the sentences below in as many ways as possible using the word in parentheses in the past tense or its base form with *used to* or *would*.

1. Marta _would listen/used to listen/listened_ (listen) to language tapes when she was on the bus.

2. When he was young, Alfonso ______________________________ (hate) studying English.

3. Jacob never ______________________________ (understand) what young children said.

4. When Greta was 15, she ______________________________ (come) to live in the United States.

5. In El Salvador, Teresa's family ______________________________ (own) a large farm.

6. When Kim finally got to Cairo, she ______________________________ (feel) relieved.

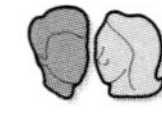

5 Evaluating a Paragraph Read the paragraph below. Then discuss it with a partner. Do you like it? Why or why not?

From the time he arrived in Beijing, Harry was obsessed with learning Chinese. He used to get up every morning before work and study for two hours. He used to listen to Chinese tapes in his car on his way to work. He used to ask everyone in the office to speak to him in Chinese even though he used to get very confused. At night, Harry used to take Chinese classes. On the weekends, he used to go to Chinese movies and listen to Chinese music. He didn't used to go out with foreigners. Unfortunately, he used to feel lonely. Finally, he met Shin Wa, and they became good friends.

▲ Chinese characters can be diffucult for westerners to learn.

6 Rewriting a Paragraph Rewrite the paragraph above. Make it less repetitive by changing *used to* to *would* or the simple past tense where appropriate.

7 Writing Sentences with *Used To* and *Would* Think about the narrative essay you are going to write. Write three sentences using *used to* or *would* that you could use in the body paragraph of your essay.

8 Writing the First Draft Write your three-paragraph narrative essay. Use the notes you've taken throughout the chapter to guide you.

Part 3 Revising and Editing

Revising for Content and Editing for Form

1 Revising for Content The first paragraph of the following narrative essay needs a topic sentence, and the last paragraph needs a concluding sentence. Read the composition. Then add a topic sentence and a concluding sentence. Then cross out any irrelevant information in the essay.

▲ When Maryam was 14, she arrived in the United States.

When Maryam was very young, she lived in a small village in Bosnia with her parents and her brothers and sisters. Her parents were farmers. They grew wheat and vegetables. At that time, there was a war in Bosnia. Sometimes her parents would talk about the war. Only a few soldiers came to Maryam's village, so her family felt safe. Maryam's older brother decided not to fight in the war. Then one day bombs began to fall on their village, and many soldiers came to fight there. Maryam's parents died in the fighting. Maryam and her sister went to live with their grandmother in the city of Sarajevo. Sarajevo used to be a beautiful city, but it was destroyed in the war. One day when Maryam was 14, their grandmother told them that they were going to go to the United States to live with their aunt.

At first, Maryam's life in the United States was very difficult. She went to an American high school, and she felt very uncomfortable there. She went to John F. Kennedy High School in Trenton, New Jersey. Learning English wasn't easy, and the other students were very different from her. Gradually, Maryam began to make friends, first with other foreign students and finally with some Americans. She learned to speak English well and became comfortable with the American way of life.

Although Maryam still thinks about her life in Bosnia, she doesn't feel homesick anymore. Maryam's sister is still planning to return to Bosnia. Today Maryam is 18 years old. When she graduates from high school, she plans to go to college to become a nurse.

PUNCTUATING SENTENCES WITH TRANSITIONS AND SUBORDINATING CONJUNCTIONS

We use transition words to connect ideas in a paragraph to make it cohesive. When transition words such as at *first*, *therefore*, *first of all*, *finally*, *in addition*, and *also* come at the beginning of a sentence, they are followed by a comma.

Examples

At first, Maryam's life in the United States was very difficult.

I couldn't speak English. I had no friends, and I was living in a terrible place. Therefore, I wanted to go home.

Transition words are different from subordinating conjunctions such as *when* and *because*. (See Appendix 5 for lists of subordinating conjunctions and Appendix 6 for lists of transition words.)

Punctuating with Subordinating Conjunctions and Subordinate Clauses

Subordinating conjunctions connect dependent clauses (or subordinate conjunctions) and independent clauses *within a sentence*. When a subordinating conjunction comes at the beginning of a sentence, a comma follows the subordinate clause that it introduces.

Subordinate Clause + comma + Independent Clause

Example

Because I was unhappy, I wanted to go home.

Because is the subordinating conjunction, and *Because I was unhappy* is the subordinate clause. It is a dependent clause.

When a subordinate clause comes in the middle or at the end of a sentence, no comma is necessary.

Independent Clause + (no comma) + Subordinate Clause

Example

I wanted to go home because I was unhappy.

2 Editing for Form Edit the following paragraph for correct punctuation around transition words and subordinating conjunctions.

May 14, 1981, was the most memorable day in my life. On that day, my family left our home in Eritrea to live in the United States. Although I was only eight years old I thought I knew what life would be like in America. Because I had seen many movies about life in the United States I remember wondering if I would be able to have a horse and carry a gun when I got there. In addition even though my father kept telling me that we were going to be living in a big city, I still imagined myself in the "Wild West."

WRITING WITH COMPUTERS

When you are writing a document that is longer than the screen, you can split the screen to view two parts of it at the same time. When you split the screen, you see two different parts of the document in two different windows. Then you can scroll through each one independently.

Evaluating Your Writing

3 Using a Rubric Read the rubric below with your class. Then use the rubric to score your essay.

Score	Description
3 **Excellent**	■ **Content:** Essay presents an interesting narrative about another person's experiences living in a foreign country. ■ **Organization:** Essay includes three paragraphs: introduction, body, and conclusion. ■ **Vocabulary:** Vocabulary is specific, varied, and used correctly throughout. ■ **Grammar:** *Used to* and *would* are used correctly, and *-ed* and *-ing* adjectives are used correctly. There are very few common grammar mistakes. ■ **Spelling and Mechanics:** Most words are spelled correctly, and punctuation is correct.
2 **Adequate**	■ **Content:** Essay presents a narrative about another person's experiences living in a foreign country, but some details may be missing or irrelevant. ■ **Organization:** Essay includes an introduction, body, and conclusion, but some information might be in the wrong paragraph. ■ **Vocabulary:** Vocabulary is specific and varied, but one or two words may be used incorrectly. ■ **Grammar:** There may be problems with *used to* and *would* or with *-ed* and *-ing* adjectives. ■ **Spelling and Mechanics:** Essay may contain some spelling and punctuation mistakes.
1 **Developing**	■ **Content:** Essay does not present a narrative about another person's experience living in a foreign country. ■ **Organization:** Essay does not include an introduction, body, and conclusion. ■ **Vocabulary:** Vocabulary is limited, and there are too many mistakes to understand or follow the ideas. ■ **Grammar:** There are many grammar mistakes, and the writing is confusing. ■ **Spelling and Mechanics:** Essay includes many distracting spelling and punctuation mistakes.

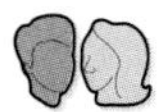

4 Peer Sharing Read your partner's narrative essay. Do you understand the story? Compare it to the essay that you wrote. How are the experiences of the two people the same? How are they different?

5 Writing the Second Draft Rewrite your essay using your rubric evaluation. Revise for content, and edit for form. Then give your essay to your teacher for comments. When your teacher returns your paper, ask him or her about any comments you don't understand.

Part 4 Expansion Activities

1 Sharing Your Writing Work in small groups. Take turns reading your narrative essays aloud.

2 Sharing Language Learning Experiences In groups, answer the following questions:

1. Have you ever been traveling and needed to get information from someone who only speaks English? What happened?
2. Have you watched movies or listened to music in English and tried to understand the words? Was it frustrating or challenging?

3 Writing in Your Journal Write in your journal for 10 or 15 minutes, answering one or both of the following questions:

1. Is it important to learn another language? Why or why not?
2. What are the difficulties in learning to speak a foreign language?

4 Researching Stories About Immigrants There are many websites on the Internet with stories by and about immigrants. Use a search engine to find some. Choose the most interesting story among the ones you find, and answer these questions:

1. What is the person's name?
2. Where did he or she come from?
3. Why did he or she immigrate?
4. How did he or she feel at first? Why?

Self-Assessment Log

In this chapter, you worked through the activities listed below. How much did they help you to become a better writer? Check *A lot, A little,* or *Not at all*.

	A lot	A little	Not at all
I interviewed a classmate about living abroad.	❑	❑	❑
I learned to use *-ed* and *-ing* adjectives to describe feelings.	❑	❑	❑
I learned to focus on one subject.	❑	❑	❑
I learned to write an introduction.	❑	❑	❑
I learned to write a conclusion.	❑	❑	❑
I learned to organize information in a three-paragraph essay.	❑	❑	❑
I learned to use gerund subjects.	❑	❑	❑
I learned to avoid problems with parallelism.	❑	❑	❑
I used a writing rubric to evaluate my first draft.	❑	❑	❑
(Add something) ______________________________	❑	❑	❑

____

Tastes and Preferences

In This Chapter

Genre Focus: Compare/Contrast

Writing Product

A comparative essay about two types of housing

Writing Process

- Practice finding bases of comparison.
- Free write to develop ideas.
- Use a comparison chart to organize ideas.
- Learn to write an introduction and conclusion for a comparison essay.
- Write about similarities with *both* and *neither.*
- Use comparatives and superlatives.
- Use *while, in contrast,* and *on the other hand.*

"Be it ever so humble, there's no place like home."

—John Howard Payne, *Home Sweet Home*
American actor and dramatist (1791–1852)

Connecting to the Topic

1. What does the photo show?
2. Have you ever had to find an apartment to rent? How did you go about it?
3. Would you prefer a different living situation than the one you have now? If so, what?

Part 1 Before You Write

Exploring Ideas

1 Discussing Living Situations As a class or in small groups, look at the photos below. Discuss the types of living situations they illustrate. How are they similar? How are they different? What kind of living situation would you prefer? What kinds don't you like? Why?

▲ Some students live in dormitories.

▲ Some students choose to rent an apartment together.

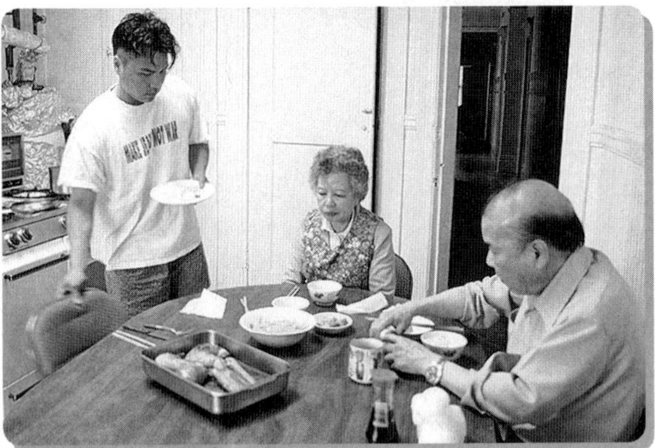

▲ Some students live at home.

2 Discussing Student Housing Options With a partner, discuss student housing situations. Describe the advantages and disadvantages of each living situation. When you finish your discussion, choose two different kinds of housing options to write about.

What Do You Think?

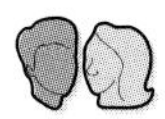

Finding Interesting Bases of Comparison

To make a comparison essay interesting, it is important to choose topics that have a strong and interesting basis of comparison. That is, even if the two things you are comparing are very different, they should have something in common that will be interesting to write about. For example, although a race car driver and the mayor of a city are both famous, *fame* is not a strong or interesting basis of comparison in this case. You would not have a lot to write about. However, if you compared the mayor of a city to the president of a company, a strong basis of comparison would be that they both run large organizations. It would be interesting to compare the two jobs based on similarities and differences in running a city and a company. In thinking of a basis of comparison, remember that some of the most interesting writing explores surprising similarities and differences.

Identifying Bases of Comparison

With a partner, decide if the things in each pair below could be compared. What are some possible bases of comparison within each pair?

1. the Nile River / New York City *tourism / danger / change over time*
2. a police officer / a coal miner ______________________
3. a baby / an old man ______________________
4. swimming / shopping ______________________
5. a mountain / a whale ______________________
6. bike riding / skiing ______________________
7. San Francisco / Riyadh ______________________
8. the Amazon River / the Mississippi River ______________________

3 Free Writing Free write for ten minutes about the two living situations that you chose in Activity 2.

4 Sharing Your Free Writing As a class, discuss your notes from Activity 3. What bases of comparison can you use to compare the two living situations you chose? Discuss the following list of characteristics. Add any others you can think of.

access to stores	privacy	expense	comfort
access to university facilities	public space	social life	safety
personal space	responsibilities		

Building Vocabulary

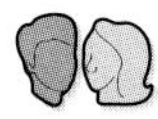

5 Using a Vocabulary Chart Below are some words that you may be able to use in your essay. Discuss them with a partner. If there are any that you don't know, look them up in a dictionary. Add words to the list that you used in your discussion in Activity 4.

Adjectives	Nouns	Verbs
accessible	chores	buy
cheap	companionship	clean
cozy	dormitory (dorm)	compromise
exorbitant	housemate	concentrate
inexpensive	landlady	cook
messy	landlord	divide
off-campus	public transportation	share
on-campus	rent	______
orderly	rooming house	______
spacious	roommate	______
tidy	utilities	______
______	solitude	______
______	______	______
______	______	______
______	______	______
______	______	______
______	______	______

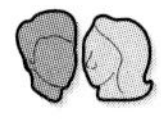

6 Discussing New Vocabulary Look at the adjectives in the chart above. With a partner, discuss whether each adjective can be used to describe a person, a place, or both.

7 Finding Antonyms Look at the adjectives in Activity 5 again. Draw arrows connecting the antonyms (opposites). Look at the adjectives that are left. Think of antonyms for those adjectives. Write the pairs of words on the lines provided.

______________________ ______________________

______________________ ______________________

______________________ ______________________

8 Categorizing Nouns Put a check mark (✔) in the correct column for each noun.

Nouns	Person	Place	Thing	
			Concrete	Not Concrete
roommate				
housemate				
companionship				
chores				
rooming house				
landlady/landlord				
utilities				
solitude				
dormitory				
public transportation				

9 Analyzing Word Parts Look at the nouns below. Think about the parts of the words, and answer the questions. Use a dictionary if you need to.

roommate housemate

1. What are the two parts of these words?
2. Can you guess the meaning of the second part?
3. Can you think of any other words that end in the second part?

landlady landlord

1. What are the two parts of these words?
2. What do the second parts of the words show?

companionship

1. What are the two parts of this word?
2. Can you think of any other words that end in the second part?

Organizing Ideas

10 Using Graphic Organizers Use the comparison chart on the next page to organize your ideas for your essay. In the first column, list three bases for comparison that you wrote in your notes for Activity 4. At the top of the middle and right columns, write the types of housing that you are going to compare. Fill in the chart on the next page.

Bases of Comparison		
privacy	not very much	a lot

11 Listing Similarities and Differences Using the information you wrote in your graphic organizer, make a list of the similarities and differences between the two living situations you chose.

Similarities

____

____

____

____

____

____

Differences

Living situation A:

____

____

____

Living situation B:

____

____

____

Look at your lists. If there are more similarities, focus on the similarities in your essay; if there are more differences, focus on the differences.

12 Analyzing an Essay Read the essay below comparing renting a room with a family and living in an apartment. Then answer the questions that follow.

When you attend a university, you have to make many decisions. Among the most important is deciding where to live. Two popular options are renting a room with a family and renting an apartment on your own or with a roommate. These living situations differ in many important ways including price, convenience, and amount of independence.

Living with a family is very different from living on your own. First of all, it is less expensive and much easier than renting an apartment. Secondly, when you live with a family, you usually eat with them, so you don't have to cook for yourself. In contrast, in your own apartment, you must do all the cooking. Finally, living with a family, you probably wouldn't be lonely because there are people to interact with. On the other hand, if you value independence, you would probably prefer to be on your own in an apartment. When you rent an apartment, you can feel free to do what you want, when you want. No one will complain if you want to watch television in the middle of the night or eat breakfast at three in the afternoon. You may also find it easier to study without any interruption.

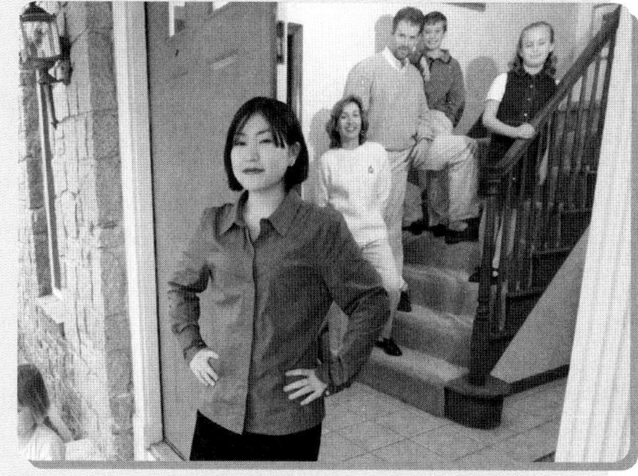

▲ Some students prefer to live with a family.

When you're deciding where to live, the differences between living in an apartment and living with a family should be considered carefully. There is no one right answer for everyone. Both living situations have advantages and disadvantages. You are the only one who can decide which would suit you best.

1. Does the essay focus more on similarities or differences?
2. What are the bases of comparison that the author has chosen?
3. In the second paragraph, what do you notice about the order the author chose to write about the bases of comparison?
4. Find the words and expressions below in the essay. Which ones does the writer use to show similarities? Which ones show differences?

both *in contrast* *less* *on the other hand*

Strategy

Writing An Introductory Paragraph

The first paragraph of an essay is the introductory paragraph. In a comparative essay, the introductory paragraph tells the reader what you are going to compare and gives an idea of how the essay is organized. The first paragraph should state:

- what you are comparing.
- your bases of comparison.
- whether you will concentrate on similarities or differences.

13 Analyzing an Introduction Look at the essay in Activity 12. Find the sections that give the information listed above.

14 Preparing to Write an Introduction Write notes for an introduction to your essay.

Strategy

Writing a Conclusion

The final paragraph of an essay is the conclusion. The conclusion usually sums up what was said in the body of the paragraph and includes an additional thought or personal opinion on the topic. The conclusion should not go off topic or introduce new ideas.

15 Analyzing a Conclusion Look at the conclusion to the essay in Activity 12. Which part summarizes what was said in the body paragraph? Which part adds new thoughts or opinions?

16 Preparing to Write a Conclusion Write notes for a conclusion for your essay.

TOEFL® IBT

Focus on Testing

Organizing Information Before You Write

In this chapter, you practiced listing similarities and differences between living situations. It is often helpful to make this kind of list before you start writing a response on a timed writing test. However, tests like the TOEFL® Internet-Based Test (iBT) usually ask you to focus specifically on differences.

The best way to plan a timed response to a question about differences is to make a table with two lists side-by-side. Each list is for one side of an issue. For example, if the prompt asks, "How do Dr. Smith's views about living situations differ from Professor Baker's?" you would make one list for Dr. Smith's views and, right beside it, another for Professor Baker's views. Read the information in the following contrast table.

Contrast Table

Prof. Baker's Views (in support of living alone)	Dr. Smith's Views (in support of living with others)
College students who live with other people get better grades in the humanities and social sciences than those who live alone.	College students who live alone get better grades in mathematics than those living with other people.
Students who live alone do not spend enough time interacting with others.	Students who live with others do not spend enough time studying.
When you live by yourself, you might let your apartment get so dirty that it is bad for your health.	When you live with other people, you have to clean the house regularly, which is a waste of time.

When you live with others, your roommates can help you if you have a problem.	If you live by yourself, you can solve problems your own way, without interference from others.
When you live with others, you will likely be exposed to other cultures.	Living alone allows you to follow your own customs in food and religion.

Practice Choose one of the three topics below. Using the contrast table as a model, create a new table including some possible differences of opinion between Smith and Baker.

1. Smith: Fun-loving students make the most of their college years.
   Baker: Serious students make the most of their college years.
2. Smith: Living in a house is perfect for students.
   Baker: Living in an apartment is perfect for students.
3. Smith: It's important to learn new customs and culture when you go away to college.

   Baker: Students should follow their own customs when they go away to college.

Part 2 Developing Writing Skills

Developing Cohesion and Clarity

WRITING ABOUT SIMILARITIES

Using *Both*

There are several different ways to use *both* in a sentence to show similarities.

1. Before nouns:

   Example

   Both living situations are safe and inexpensive.
2. As a pronoun:

   Example

   Both are safe and inexpensive.
3. With verbs:

   Examples

   They are both safe and inexpensive. (*Both* follows the verb *be*.)

   They have both given me a lot. (*Both* comes between the helping verb and the main verb.)

   They both offer convenience. (*Both* comes before one-word verbs except *be*.)

Using *Neither*

You can use *neither* to show negative similarities. Note that *neither* is always singular.

1. With *nor:*

   Example

   Neither living in a dorm nor sharing an apartment is ideal.

2. Before a singular noun:

   Example

   Neither situation is ideal.

3. As a pronoun:

   Example

   Neither is ideal.

---

1 Writing Sentences with *Both* and *Neither* Write sentences about the rules and facilities at a rooming house and a dormitory using *both* or *neither.* (Note: a rooming house is a house where several students rent rooms. The landlord or landlady lives in the home too. Students do their own cooking.)

1. allow / smoking

   Neither the dormitory nor the rooming house allows smoking.

2. have / kitchen

   ____

3. play / loud music

   ____

4. television / available

   ____

5. allow / visitors of the opposite sex

   ____

6. require permission / overnight guests

   ____

2 Writing Sentences with *Both* and *Neither* Write two sentences about the similarities of the living situations you chose. Use *both* or *neither.*

WRITING ABOUT DIFFERENCES

Comparatives

To compare two people or things, use one of the following patterns:
adjective + *-er* + *than* or *more/less* + adjective (+ *than*).

Examples	Notes
A rooming house is cheaper than a dorm. (A rooming house is cheaper.)	One-syllable adjectives usually take the *-er* (+ *than*) ending.
Paul is happier than Jack is about living in a dorm.	With two-syllable adjectives that end in *-y*, change the *y* to *i* before adding *-er.*
An apartment is more expensive than a dorm. (An apartment is more expensive.)	Most adjectives that have two or more syllables and don't end in *y* take *more* or *less* (+ *than*).
Apartments are better than dorms. Living in a dorm is worse than living at home.	Some irregular comparatives include *good-better; bad-worse; far-farther/further*

Superlatives

To compare three or more nouns, use these patterns:
the + adjective + *-est* or *the* + *most/least* + adjective.

Examples	Notes
Home is the cheapest accommodation you can find.	One-syllable adjectives usually take the *-est* ending.
Living in a dormitory is often the easiest.	For two-syllable adjectives that end in *y*: change the *y* to *i* before adding *-est.*
For many students, apartment life is the most difficult. A dorm is the least private.	Most adjectives with more than one syllable that don't end in *y* take the *most/least.*
Living in an apartment is the best situation for independent people. Living at home is the worst choice if you want to be independent.	Irregular superlatives include *the best*; *the worst*; *the farthest/furthest.*

3 Completing Sentences with Comparatives and Superlatives

Complete the sentences below using the comparative or superlative forms of the adjectives in parentheses.

1. A rooming house is more economical (economical) than an apartment.
2. Of all the possibilities, students probably feel ____________ (independent) in an apartment.
3. Even though there are police on most campuses, it's hard to say that living on campus is ____________ (safe) than living off campus.

4. My room is small but it's ___________________ (cozy) than my room in the dorm.
5. For many people, dorm life is the ___________________ (stressful) of all the options.
6. Sharing an apartment with a few other students can be ___________________ (cheap) than living in a dorm.
7. Staying in a dormitory on campus is usually the ___________________ (convenient) living situation because you are close to classes.
8. I have lived in a dorm, an apartment, and at home. I thought that the dorm was the ___________________ (good) situation for me.
9. Many parents think that living in a dorm is ___________________ (safe) than living in an apartment.
10. Dormitory food is often ___________________ (bad) than food you can cook yourself, even if you are not a great cook.

USING *WHILE*

You can use *while* to show two different or opposite ideas in a sentence. If *while* comes at the beginning of the sentence, use a comma at the end of the clause it introduces.

The subject of the clause with *while* should be the same as the subject of the second clause in the sentence.

Example

While living at home is inexpensive, it may cause you to miss out on social opportunities.

In the first clause, *living at home* is the subject. In the second clause, *it* is the subject. *It* clearly refers to *living at home.*

---

4 Rewriting Sentences Using *While*

Rewrite the sentences below with *while.*

1. Although you may want to live at home so that you don't have to do housework, you may feel too dependent if you are not on your own.

   While you may want to live at home so that you don't have to do housework, you may feel too dependent if you are not on your own.

2. A dorm can be a fun place to live, but it is not always the best place to study.

   ____

   ____

3. Although some roommates get along very well, others argue a lot.

   ____

   ____

4. Apartment living may sound like fun, but the reality of it can be quite different.

____

____

5. Although I don't mind cooking for myself, I hate cleaning my apartment.

____

____

▲ Many students live in dormitories.

5 Writing Sentences with *While* Look at the following lists showing the differences between living in a dormitory and living in an apartment or with a family. On the lines below, write three sentences with *while* to show the differences.

Living in a Dormitory	Living in an Apartment or with a Family
■ is less expensive	■ may require a long commute
■ don't have household chores	■ feel part of the community
■ must share a room	■ it's possible to have a room to yourself
■ are never lonely	■ may feel separated from campus life
■ must eat cafeteria food	■ can cook your own food or go to restaurants

1. *While living in a dormitory is less expensive, it may be more convenient than living in an apartment or with a family because you'll be closer to campus.*

2. ____

3. ____

4. ____

USING EXPRESSIONS OF CONTRAST: *IN CONTRAST* AND *ON THE OTHER HAND*

You can use the expressions *in contrast* and *on the other hand* to show contrast between two different ideas.

Examples	Notes
In contrast:	
Renting an apartment can be expensive. In contrast, living at home is inexpensive.	*In contrast* is used to contrast two different or opposite things.
Living at home is inexpensive. Renting an apartment, in contrast, is expensive.	For variety, you can use *in contrast* after the subject; if you do, use two commas.
On the other hand:	
An apartment gives you privacy. On the other hand, it can be lonely to live on your own. Renting a room in a house is more expensive. On the other hand, you have few household responsibilities.	*On the other hand* is often used to contrast advantages and disadvantages of the same thing: an apartment in the first example and renting a room in the second example.

6 Rewriting Sentences Using *In Addition, In Contrast,* and *On the Other Hand*

Rewrite the following sentences using *in addition* to show similarities. Use *in contrast* or *on the other hand* to show contrast.

1. Living in a dorm means that you are always surrounded by people. Apartment life can be quite lonely.

   Living in a dorm means that you are always surrounded by people. In contrast, apartment life can be quite lonely.

2. A rooming house is a good solution for those who like small groups of people. It's cheaper than living in a dormitory.

   ____

3. In an apartment, you can usually cook your own meals. In a dorm, you usually have to eat cafeteria food or go to restaurants.

   ____

4. Living in a dorm is an exciting new experience. Staying at home with your family is just like being in high school.

   ____

5. Living with another family can be awkward. It's less expensive than living in an apartment.

____

____

7 Completing Sentences

Complete the following sentences.

1. Having your own apartment can be a lot of work. In contrast,
   you don't have to do much work when you rent a room from a family.

____

2. Apartments are often expensive. On the other hand,

____

____

3. Rooming houses usually only have a few students. In contrast,

____

____

4. Cooking your own food can be an advantage. On the other hand,

____

____

5. Students who live in apartments have a lot of responsibilities. In contrast,

____

____

8 Writing the First Draft

Write your essay using the notes and organization you came up with earlier in the chapter. Use *both* and *neither* to show similarities. Use *while, in contrast,* and *on the other hand* to show differences. Use *however* and *although* to show contrast.

▲ Students in dormitories don't cook for themselves.

Part 3 Revising and Editing

Revising for Content and Editing for Form

1 Revising for Content Improve the flow of the first sample body paragraph by adding *however* and *in addition* where appropriate. Improve the flow of the second sample body paragraph by adding *while* and *in contrast* where appropriate.

My home is in the old section of Cairo. My neighborhood is a mass of tiny streets surrounded on all sides by thousands of years of history. I live very near the university where my father teaches. He teaches Islamic history, so I know a lot about the place where I live. His students often come to visit us. My house is hundreds of years old, and it looks it. The rooms are small and dark. The kitchen has few modern appliances. The water supply is also unpredictable except when it rains. Then the roof always leaks—somewhere. We have a sun-filled courtyard full of beautiful flowers. Even on the hottest days, the thick mud and stone walls keep us cool and comfortable. Living in my neighborhood, I can never forget where I came from. I am literally surrounded by history.

My cousin Sai'id has a very different home. He lives in one of the newest sections of Cairo. I live in the past. Sai'id is very much in the present. His neighborhood is full of office towers, trendy shops, and every American fast food restaurant imaginable. Sai'id's favorite fast food is hamburgers, but I prefer fried chicken. My father works in the world's oldest university. Sai'id's father works for a new communications company. His family lives in a modern apartment building. Their large, air-conditioned apartment contains almost every kind of modern appliance. In my family, we spend our evenings reading. Sai'id's family gathers around their large-screen TV. I enjoy visiting Sai'id, but I am always happy to return to the comfort of old Cairo.

2 Editing for Form Identify and correct the mistakes in the use of comparatives and superlatives in the paragraph below.

more convenient

The decision about whether to live on or off campus is a very important one. It could affect your entire college career. Both situations have advantages and disadvantages, and which one you choose depends a lot on what is important to you. For example, on-campus housing is generally much ~~convenienter~~ than off-campus housing. It's more easy to get to class, especially early in the morning. Students who live on campus are also more closer to facilities such as the library and gym. On the other hand, in a dorm, you usually have to share a room, while off-campus housing can be much more private and least noisy. Cafeteria food is another disadvantage of on-campus housing. Students on special diets will often find it difficult to live in a dormitory than to live in a rooming house or apartment where they can cook for themselves.

Evaluating Your Writing

3 Using a Rubric Read the rubric below with your class. Then use the rubric to score your essay.

Score	Description
3 **Excellent**	■ **Content:** Essay compares two types of housing and includes bases of comparison and details about similarities and differences. ■ **Organization:** Introduction includes bases of comparison. Body paragraph compares housing options. Conclusion sums up the essay and includes additional thoughts or opinions. ■ **Vocabulary:** Vocabulary is specific, and expressions of similarities and differences are used correctly. ■ **Grammar:** Gerunds, comparatives, and superlatives are used correctly. ■ **Spelling and Mechanics:** Words are spelled correctly, and punctuation is correct.

2 **Adequate**	▪ **Content:** Essay compares two types of housing, but bases of comparison and details about similarities and differences may be limited. ▪ **Organization:** Some necessary items from the introduction, body paragraph, and conclusion may be missing. ▪ **Vocabulary:** Vocabulary is clear, but the essay may include some mistakes in expressions of similarities and differences. ▪ **Grammar:** Most gerunds, comparatives, and superlatives are used correctly. ▪ **Spelling and Mechanics:** Essay includes some spelling or punctuation mistakes.
1 **Developing**	▪ **Content:** Essay doesn't compare two types of housing or does not include bases of comparison, and details about similarities and differences are missing. ▪ **Organization:** Essay does not have three paragraphs, and many items from the introduction, body paragraph, and conclusion may be missing. ▪ **Vocabulary:** Vocabulary is limited, and there are too many mistakes to understand the ideas. ▪ **Grammar:** Gerunds, comparatives, and superlatives are not used or are used incorrectly throughout. ▪ **Spelling and Mechanics:** Essay includes many distracting spelling and punctuation mistakes.

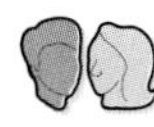

4 Peer Sharing Exchange papers with another student. Answer the following questions about your partner's essay:

1. What does the essay compare?
2. What are the bases of comparison?
3. Does the essay focus on similarities or differences, or both?
4. Do you agree with the author? Discuss any differences of opinion.

WRITING WITH COMPUTERS

You can set your word processing program to find punctuation problems. However, you should always check the computer's changes to make sure they are correct in each case. A computer cannot check grammar reliably.

5 Writing the Second Draft Rewrite your essay using your rubric evaluation. Revise for content, and edit for form. Then give your essay to your teacher for comments. When your teacher returns your paper, ask him or her about any comments you don't understand.

Part 4 Expansion Activities

1 Evaluating A Comparison Find a comparison of two things or two people in a newspaper, magazine, or website. Note the words and expressions the writer uses in the comparison. Is he or she focusing mainly on differences or similarities?

2 Comparing Two Movies Write a paragraph comparing two movies that you have seen. When you finish, give your paragraph to a partner to read.

3 Writing in Your Journal Write in your journal for 15 minutes about one or both of the following topics.

1. The similarities and differences between your high school and your college
2. A comparison of two things or two people: types of music, cities, kinds of transportation, politicians, anything that has a basis for comparison

4 Researching Housing Options Go to a university website. Remember most colleges and universities have the Internet address *www.nameofuniversity.edu*. On the site, search for housing or student life. Find out what kinds of housing are available. Which would you prefer and why?

Self-Assessment Log

In this chapter, you worked through the activities listed below. How much did they help you to become a better writer? Check *A lot, A little,* or *Not at all*.

	A lot	A little	Not at all
I practiced finding bases of comparison.	❑	❑	❑
I used free writing to generate ideas for my essay.	❑	❑	❑
I used a comparison chart to organize my ideas.	❑	❑	❑
I learned to write an introduction and conclusion for a comparison essay.	❑	❑	❑
I used *both* and *neither* to write about similarities.	❑	❑	❑
I practiced using comparatives and superlatives.	❑	❑	❑
I learned to use *while, in contrast,* and *on the other hand.*	❑	❑	❑
I used a writing rubric to evaluate my first draft.	❑	❑	❑
(Add something) ______________________________	❑	❑	❑
______________________________			

New Frontiers

In This Chapter

Genre Focus: Descriptive

Writing Product

A descriptive essay about a planet

Writing Process

- Get information from charts and tables.
- Speculate about a topic.
- Use a graphic organizer to arrange ideas.
- Order information in a descriptive essay.
- Use the passive voice.
- Vary sentence structure by using *with* or *unlike* + noun phrase.
- Give reasons with *because* and *because of*.

“Astronomy compels the soul to look upwards and leads us from this world to another.”

—Plato
Greek philosopher (428–347 BC)

Connecting to the Topic

1. Are you interested in astronomy?
2. Would you like to travel in space? Why or why not?
3. Do you think there is life on other planets? Why or why not?

Part 1 A Before You Write

Exploring Ideas

1 Getting Information from Tables Look at Table 1 below and the chart on the next page. Answer the following questions.

1. Which planet is the largest? ______________________
2. Which planet has the most moons? ______________________
3. Which planet is the farthest from the sun? ______________________
4. Which planet revolves around the sun the most slowly? ______________________
5. Which planet revolves around the sun the most quickly? ______________________
6. How many moons does Neptune have? ______________________
7. Which planet is the hottest? ______________________
8. Which planet is the coldest? ______________________

Table 1

Planet	Diameter (in miles)	Number of Moons	Distance from Sun (in millions of miles)	Revolution Around Sun
Mercury	3,032	0	36	88 days
Venus	7,523	0	67	224.7 days
Earth	7,928	1	92.9	365.26 days
Mars	4,218	2	141.5	687 days
Jupiter	88,900	63	483.4	4,331 days
Saturn	74,900	47	884.6	10,747 days
Uranus	31,800	27	1783.8	30, 589 days
Neptune	30,800	13	2793.9	59, 800 days

* one mile = 1.61 kilometers

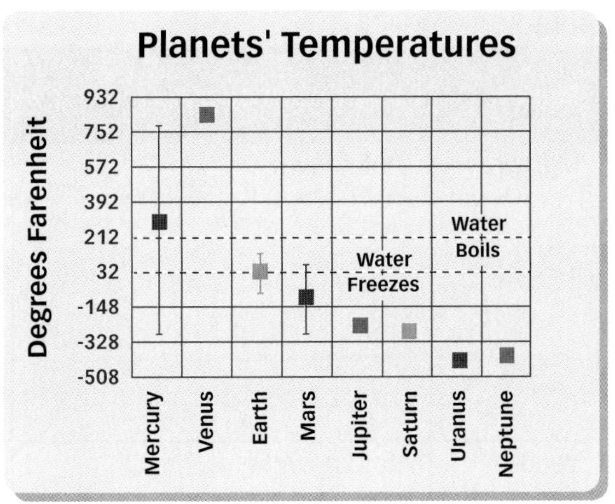

2 **Getting Information from Tables** Look at Table 2 below and 3 on the next page. Answer the following questions:

1. When was Uranus discovered? ____________________
2. Which planets have been visited by spacecraft? ____________________
3. What is the atmosphere of Mars made of? ____________________
4. What is an interesting feature of Jupiter? ____________________
5. Which planets have rings? ____________________

Table 2

Planet	Composition of Atmosphere	Features
Mercury	little or none	craters like the moon
Venus	carbon dioxide	220 mile per hour winds, daytime temperature of 800 degrees
Earth	nitrogen, oxygen	
Mars	carbon dioxide, nitrogen, argon	bright red color, some evidence of water.
Jupiter	hydrogen, helium	Great Red Spot 25,000 miles long, several rings, 63 moons
Saturn	hydrogen, helium	huge system of rings of rock and ice.
Uranus	hydrogen, helium, methane	11 rings and 27 moons
Neptune	hydrogen, helium, methane	high winds and rocky core

* In 2006, Pluto was reclassified from a planet to a dwarf planet.

Table 3

Planet	Planet Discovery	Exploration and New Discoveries
Mercury	not known	In 1975, Mariner 310 found a magnetic field that surprised scientists. In 2004 the MESSENGER spacecraft was launched. It will enter Mercury's orbit in 2011 and orbit the planet for one year.
Venus	not known	The European Space Agency launched Venus Express in November 2005. It will map the surface.
Mars	not known	Mars Rover 2003 found evidence of water. In August 2005 Mars Reconnaissance Orbiter was launched to search for evidence of ancient seas.
Jupiter	not known	Pioneers 10 and 11 sent back photographs in 1975; Voyagers 1 and 2 sent back moving pictures in 1979. Galileo spacecraft sent a probe to the surface in 1989 to get information on temperature, pressure, and chemical composition.
Saturn	not known	Cassini was launched in 1997 and is currently orbiting Saturn.
Uranus	Sir William Herschel, 1781	Voyager 2 sent back pictures in 1986; discovered 10 new moons and strong magnetic field.
Neptune	Johann Galle, 1846	Voyager 2 flew by in 1989; discovered 3 rings and 6 new moons.

3 Choosing a Planet to Write About Select a planet other than Earth or Uranus to write about. Study the information in Activities 1 and 2, and complete the chart below. Look on the Internet to find more information.

Name: ______________________

Size: ______________________

Distance from the sun: ______________________

Composition: ______________________

Rotation: ______________________

Revolution around the sun: ______________________

Discovered: ______________________

Exploration / New discoveries: ______________________

Moons: ______________________

Interesting features: ______________________

Other: ______________________

What Do You Think?

Speculating

When you speculate about a subject, you make a guess based on what you already know about it. Making speculations is useful when you are writing about a topic that has ongoing importance in scientific, social, and political matters.

Making Speculations

Practice speculating by answering the questions below about the planet you chose. Then share your answers with a partner.

1. Can the planet support life? Why or why not?
2. What information helped you answer this question?

Building Vocabulary

4 Using a Vocabulary Chart The chart on the next page contains words used to discuss planets. Review the lists and look up any words you don't know. Add any other words that you think belong in this category. Think of words you used to answer the questions in previous activities.

Nouns	Verbs	Adjectives
atmosphere	be composed of	dense
composition	discover	frozen
crater	explore	inhabited
diameter	inhabit	inner
discoverer	orbit	outer
discovery	revolve	poisonous
exploration	rotate	rocky
explorer		uninhabited
orbit		
revolution		
rotation		

5 Matching Words to Their Definitions Work with a partner. Read the definitions, and find the words in the list above. Then write the word on the line.

1. Find something new _discover_______________

   A person who finds something new ____________________

   The thing that the person finds ____________________

2. To live in a place ____________________

   Not supporting life ____________________

3. Travel through an unfamiliar place ____________________

   To get information about it ____________________

   A person who does this ____________________

   The act of doing this ____________________

6 **Using New Vocabulary** Look at the drawings below. Which shows a planet's revolution around the sun? Which shows a planet rotating?

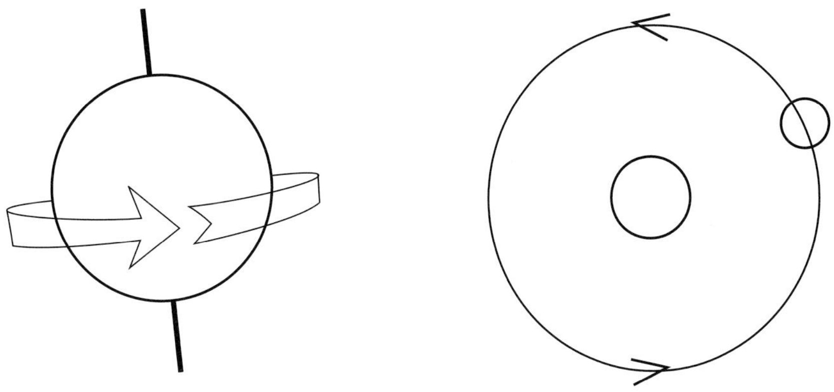

7 **Using New Vocabulary** Look at the drawings below. Which line is the diameter?

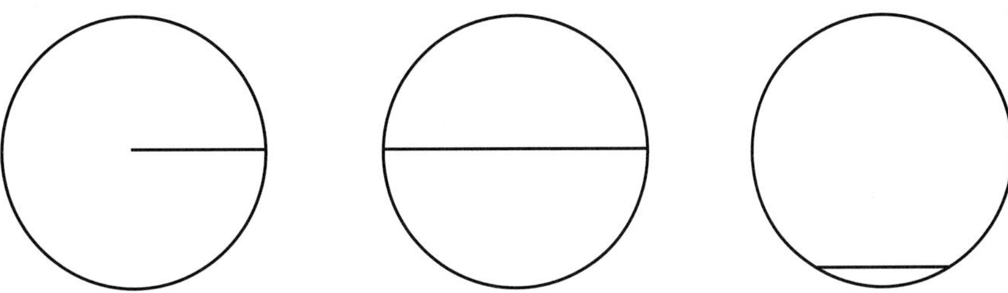

8 **Discussing New Vocabulary** In small groups, answer the following questions about the vocabulary words:

1. What is the function of the suffix *-tion* in the following pairs of words?

compose	composition
explore	exploration
revolve	revolution
rotate	rotation

2. Can you think of any other nouns that end in *-tion*? Do they have related verbs?
3. What is the function of the suffix *-ous* in the following pairs of words?

danger	dangerous
gas	gaseous
poison	poisonous

4. Can you think of any other adjectives that end in *-ous*?
5. What is the function of the suffix *-ed* in the following pair of words?

inhabit	inhabited

9 Discussing Expressions In writing about a planet, you will need to use expressions to describe the planet's position, movements, and composition. Discuss the list of expressions below in groups.

Location/Motion

is surrounded by
lies between
passes by / passes close to
revolves around

Composition

is composed of
is made up of (more than one item)
is made of (only one item)

WRITING WITH COMPUTERS

Did you know that you can create tables and charts in your document? Look on the toolbar of your word processing program for the **insert table** command, or click **help** and do a search for **create table**.
You can specify the number of rows and columns you want. You can also add or delete rows and columns. However, if you do this you will lose the information in those spaces.

Organizing Ideas

10 Describing a Planet One way to organize your descriptive essay is to describe how the planet you are writing about is different from Earth or the other planets. Look at your notes. Compare the planet you chose to Earth. List some of the similarities and differences.

Using Graphic Organizers

11 Analyzing a Graphic Organizer The graphic organizer below contains some of the information that one student found about Uranus. Study the diagram. What shape is used for the topic? What shape is used for the subtopics? What shape is used for the details?

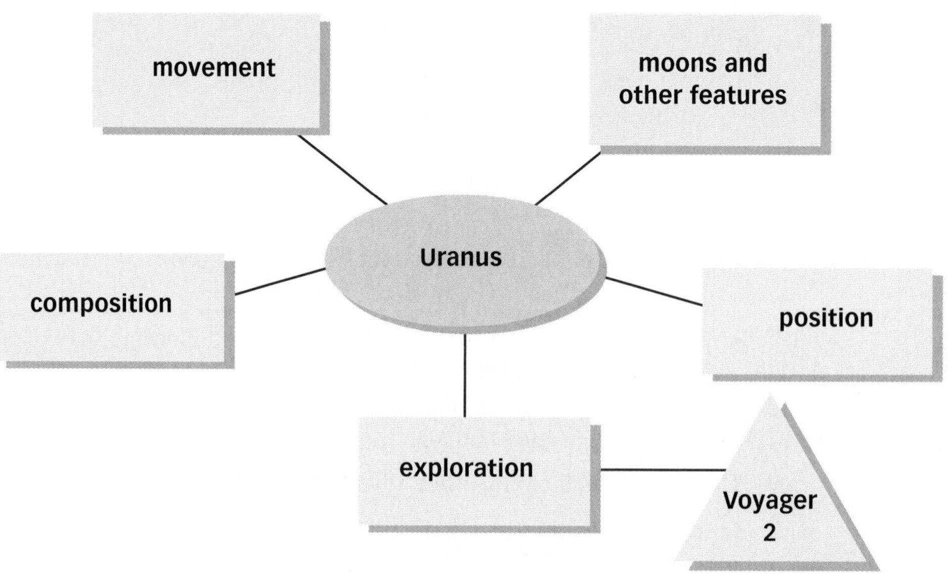

12 **Completing a Graphic Organizer** The essay below was written using information from the graphic organizer on page 164. Read the essay, and add information to the graphic organizer with information from the essay.

Uranus is one of the most mysterious planets in the solar system. It is 1783 million miles from the sun. That is about 19 times farther from the sun than the Earth. Uranus was discovered in 1781 by the British astronomer Sir William Herschel. He first saw Uranus with a telescope, but from a dark site, it can be seen with the naked eye. For 200 years not much was known about Uranus. Then in 1986 the Voyager 2 spaceship passed by Uranus and took pictures.

Along with Jupiter, Saturn, and Neptune, Uranus is known as one of the gas giants—very large planets made up almost entirely of vapor and frozen gas. Uranus is almost four times the size of Earth, and its orbit is much larger. It takes this planet 84 Earth-years to complete its trip around the sun. However, a day on Uranus is shorter than a day on Earth. It lasts only 17 hours. Scientific studies have now shown that the atmosphere of Uranus is composed of hydrogen, helium, and methane and has a temperature of approximately –270°F. Uranus has 11 rings and 27 moons.

We still know little about the seventh planet from the Earth, but other unmanned space missions are planned to explore our very distant neighbor. Who knows what mysteries Uranus has yet to reveal?

13 **Creating a Graphic Organizer** Create a graphic organizer like the one on page 164. Fill it in with information about the planet you chose.

Strategy

Ordering the Information in a Descriptive Essay

Your essay should have an introduction, a body paragraph, and a conclusion. The introduction gives general information about the subject and should entice the reader. The body paragraph should contain details describing the subject.The details should be grouped together by subtopic. The conclusion can "wrap up" or summarize what was said in the essay. It can also look to the future or include a personal opinion.

14 **Analyzing the Organization of an Essay** Read the essay on page 165 again. In the chart below, put a check (✔) next to each topic showing where you can find it in the essay. With a partner, discuss why the writer chose this order.

	Paragraph 1	Paragraph 2	Paragraph 3
position in solar system	✓		
atmosphere			
orbit			
moons / rings			
past exploration			
Saturn			
size			
revolution around the sun			
year discovered			
future exploration			

15 **Creating an Idea Chart** Create a chart similar to the one above. Show the order in which you will present information about your planet. Share your chart with a partner and discuss your ordering decisions.

▲ A view of Earth from outer space

Part 2 Developing Writing Skills

Developing Cohesion and Clarity

USING THE PASSIVE VOICE

The passive voice is used in both spoken and written English. It is often used in scientific or technical writing.

Active versus Passive Voice

In sentences in the active voice, the main focus is on the subject (the agent or doer of the action). In the passive voice, the main focus is on the person or thing acted upon rather than the person or thing that does the action. Compare the following:

Active Voice	Eight planets orbit the sun. **subject** **agent**	Main Focus = nine planets
Passive Voice	The sun is orbited by eight planets. **subject** **agent**	Main Focus = the sun

Forming the Passive Voice

All passive voice sentences contain a form of *be* + the past participle of the main verb.

By + agent can be used in a passive voice sentence to tell who or what performed the action. *By* + agent is used in a passive sentence only when the agent is important.

Examples	Notes
Active Sir William Herschel discovered Uranus.	
Passive Uranus was discovered by Sir William Herschel.	The subject *Sir William Herschel* is important; it cannot be omitted.
Active People make telescopes with a series of lenses.	
Passive Telescopes are made with a series of lenses.	The subject *people* is obvious. It is not important to the sentence. It is not necessary to add *by people* to this sentence.

Note: The following verbs are often used in the passive voice:

- The moon is not composed of cheese.
- Satellites are used to explore space.
- She is known for her scientific discoveries.

---

1 Completing a Paragraph with Active and Passive Forms of Verbs

Complete the following paragraph with the appropriate passive or active forms of the verbs in parentheses.

The Moon

The moon ___orbits___ (1) (orbit) the Earth the way the Earth __________ (2) (orbit) the sun. Scientists believe that the moon __________ (3) (form) at about the same time as the Earth.They now know that it __________ (4) (make up of) many of the same materials as the Earth. But scientists __________ (5) (find) that the moon is different from the Earth in many ways. For example, the moon __________ (6) (have) no atmosphere to carry sound; as a result, no matter what __________ (7) (happen) on the moon's surface, no sound __________ (8) (hear). Without an atmosphere, water __________ (9) (disappear) into space. That is why no water can __________ (10) (find) on the surface of the moon, although some water __________ (11) (trap) inside rocks. Without water, there can __________ (12) (be) no weather. So if you go to the moon, you will never __________ (13) (see) a cloud, __________ (14) (get) wet in a rainstorm, or __________ (15) (feel) the wind blow.

▲ A view of the moon.

2 **Writing Sentences with the Passive Voice** Look at the notes you made for your descriptive essay. Write three sentences in the passive voice about your planet.

VARYING SENTENCE STRUCTURE

Using *With* + Noun Phrase

You can make your writing more interesting by varying the sentence structure. For example, you can occasionally begin a sentence with a phrase using *with* + noun phrase. When you use this type of phrase, you must make sure that the noun modified by the phrase comes directly after the phrase. Compare the following:

Incorrect: With a temperature of 800°F, no life could survive on Venus.

Correct: With a temperature of 800°F, Venus is much too hot for life to survive.

The second sentence is correct because Venus (not life) has a temperature of 800°F.

---

3 **Matching Sentence Parts** Match the phrases in Column A with the clauses in Column B. Use the tables at the beginning of the chapter if necessary.

	A	B
1. d	With its beautiful rings,	**a.** Mars has interested astronomers for a long time.
2. ____	With a diameter of only 1,400 miles,	**b.** Venus cannot support life.
3. ____	With a daytime temperature of 800°F,	**c.** Earth looks like a blue ball from space.
4. ____	With its bright red color and changing surface features,	**d.** Saturn is the most spectacular planet in the solar system.
5. ____	With its large oceans,	**e.** Pluto is a dwarf planet.

4 **Writing a Sentence Using *With* + Noun Phrase** Write a sentence about your planet using *with* + noun phrase.

Example *With a temperature of 800 °F, Venus does not support life.*

▲ A view of the moon

USING *UNLIKE* + NOUN PHRASE

Another way to vary sentence structure is to begin a sentence with *Unlike* + noun phrase. With this phrase, you can contrast the planet you are writing about to Earth or other planets.

Example

Unlike the other planets, Venus rotates from west to east.
Unlike Earth, Mercury has no atmosphere.

Note that when you begin a sentence with *unlike*, you must use a comma at the end of the phrase it introduces.

---

5 Comparing Planets with *Unlike* Use the tables at the beginning of the chapter to complete each of the following sentences.

1. Unlike Earth, Mars has no atmosphere.
2. Unlike Earth, Jupiter ______________________
3. Unlike the other planets, Mercury ______________________
4. Unlike the other planets, Mars ______________________

GIVING REASONS WITH *BECAUSE OF* + NOUN PHRASE AND *BECAUSE* + CLAUSE

You have already learned how to use *because* to connect two clauses.

Example

No one can live on Mercury because it is very hot.

The phrase *because of* introduces a noun phrase rather than a clause.

Example

No one can live on Mercury because of its high temperature.

Note that in the first example *because* is followed by a subject and a verb, but in the second example *because of* is followed by a noun phrase. Both *because* and *because of* can be used in the middle or at the beginning of a sentence. When you begin a sentence with *because* and *because of*, you need to put a comma after the clause or phrase it introduces.

Example

Pluto's distance from the sun changes because it has an irregular orbit.
Because it has an irregular orbit, Pluto's distance from the sun changes.

Pluto's distance from the sun changes because of its irregular orbit.
Because of its irregular orbit, Pluto's distance from the sun changes.

6 Matching Sentence Parts Add *because of* or *because* to the phrases and clauses in Column A. Then match the sentence parts in Column A and Column B to make sentences.

A	B
1. Because of its irregular orbit, d .	a. Uranus takes 84 Earth-years to travel around the sun.
2. ________ its distance from the sun, ____ .	b. scientists saw the surface of Pluto for the first time.
3. ________ a desire to learn more about the solar system, ____ .	c. Pluto is extremely cold.
4. ________ our need for oxygen, ____ .	d. Pluto's distance from the sun changes.
5. ________ it is close to Earth, ____ .	e. many spaceships have been launched.
6. ________ its orbit is much larger than Earth's, ____ .	f. Mars has always interested sky-watchers.
7. ________ pictures taken by the Hubble telescope, ____ .	g. human beings could not live on Mars.

7 Writing Sentences with *Because* and *Because of* Write one sentence about your planet using *because* and one sentence using *because of.*

8 Writing the First Draft Write your descriptive essay using the information and notes you've gathered throughout this chapter. Use the passive voice when necessary, and vary the sentence structure by using *unlike* + noun phrase and *with* + noun phrase. Give reasons with *because* or *because of.*

Part 3 Revising and Editing

Revising for Content and Editing for Form

1 Revising for Content The author of the essay below found some more information about Uranus and decided to incorporate it into her first draft. Decide where to put the new information. She also found one piece of information that was incorrect. What does she need to change?

- Uranus is a blue-green color.
- 80% of Uranus is ice.
- Herschel first thought it was a comet.
- Uranus has 27 moons, not 15!

Don't worry about grammatical errors for now.

Uranus is the seventh planet in the solar system. It discovered in 1781 by the British astronomer Sir William Herschel. He first saw Uranus with a telescope, but from a dark site, it can be see with the naked eye. For 200 years not much were known about Uranus. Then in 1986, the Voyager 2 spaceship was passed by Uranus and took pictures that gave scientists much valuable information.

Unlike the terrestrial planets, that have a solid surface, Uranus is a gas giant. Gas giants very large planets made up almost entirely of vapor and frozen gas. Uranus is almost four times the size of Earth and its orbit is much larger. Because this planet large orbit it takes 84 Earth-years to complete its trip around the sun. However, a day on Uranus is shorter than a day on Earth. It lasts only 17 hours. Scientific studies have now shown that the atmosphere of Uranus composing of hydrogen, helium, and methane and has a temperature of approximately –270°F. The Voyager 2 pictures also showed that Uranus has ten rings and 15 moons.

We still know little about the seventh planet from the Earth, but other unmanned space missions planned to explore our very distant neighbor.

2 Editing Practice Edit the essay above for errors in the use of the passive voice and connectors such as *with*, *because*, and *because of*, and rewrite it correctly. Make any other corrections you feel are necessary.

Evaluating Your Writing

3 **Using a Rubric** Read the rubric below with your class. Then use the rubric to score your essay.

Score	Description
3 **Excellent**	■ **Content:** Essay describes a planet and gives important, relevant, and interesting information. ■ **Organization:** Content is organized into a cohesive introduction, body paragraph, and conclusion. Related details are grouped together. ■ **Vocabulary:** Vocabulary is specific and varied. Descriptive expressions are used correctly. ■ **Grammar:** Sentence structures are varied. Passive voice is used correctly, and verbs tenses are correct. ■ **Spelling and Mechanics:** Words are spelled correctly, and punctuation is correct.
2 **Adequate**	■ **Content:** Essay describes a planet, but some details may be lacking or irrelevant. ■ **Organization:** Content is organized into an introduction, body paragraph, and conclusion, but the order of some information within the body paragraph may not be clear. ■ **Vocabulary:** Vocabulary is mostly correct, but some specificity or variety may be lacking. ■ **Grammar:** Sentence structure is somewhat varied. Passive voice is mostly used correctly, and most verb tenses are correct. ■ **Spelling and Mechanics:** Most words are spelled correctly, and punctuation is correct.
1 **Developing**	■ **Content:** Essay does not present much information about a planet. ■ **Organization:** Essay does not contain three paragraphs, or organization may be unclear. ■ **Vocabulary:** There are too many mistakes to understand and follow the ideas. ■ **Grammar:** Sentence structure is not varied. Passive voice is not used. Many grammar mistakes make ideas difficult to follow. ■ **Spelling and Mechanics:** Essay includes distracting spelling and punctuation mistakes.

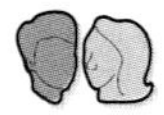

4 Peer Sharing Find another student who wrote about the same planet that you did. Compare your essays, and answer the following questions:

1. Did you use the same or similar order of information within the paragraphs?
2. Does your information agree?
3. Did one of you include information that the other did not?

5 Writing the Second Draft Rewrite your essay using your rubric evaluation. Revise for content, and edit for form. Then give your essay to your teacher for comments. When your teacher returns your paper, ask him or her about any comments you don't understand.

TOEFL® iBT

Focus on Testing

Writing Descriptions

The integrated writing prompt on the TOEFL® Internet-Based Test (iBT) may ask you to describe a process or an object. This description will be based on a brief reading and lecture.

Before you see the prompt for an integrated writing task on the TOEFL® iBT, you will receive information from two sources: (1) a reading passage that stays on your screen for 3 minutes and (2) a recorded lecture that runs about 2 minutes and 30 seconds. The prompt will ask you to use information from both sources to write about an aspect of the topic.

Practice Below is a sample reading and a transcript of a sample lecture. They are the same length as what you would see and hear on the TOEFL® iBT. Read them. Then give yourself 20 minutes to plan, write, and revise your response to the prompt that follows.

Reading

No one knew it then, but the Earth was nearly hit by an asteroid in June 2002. Astronomers didn't discover it until five days after the near-collision. That was when they finally saw the piece of space rock as it sped away from our planet. This asteroid, known as 2002 MN, is one of several "Near Earth Objects" (NEOs) being tracked by astronomers around the world.

NEOs are common, and they hit Earth's atmosphere daily. Most of them burn up when they enter the atmosphere. Scientists are interested in the big ones, which could actually do damage. Most researchers believe that the last big NEO to make it through the atmosphere was a huge asteroid that exploded in 1808 before it hit Earth's surface. It was so close to the surface that when it exploded, it flattened millions of trees in northeastern Russia.

Most NEOs are pieces of rock from the Kuiper Belt, a large area between the planets Mars and Jupiter. NEOs are pushed out of their usual place by gravitational forces from the planets. If an NEO's track crosses Earth's orbit, the NEO and Earth could collide.

The National Aeronautics and Space Administration (NASA) has assigned a team of astronomers to discover and track NEOs. This is not an easy job because many NEOs cannot be seen. Some are too small. Others are hidden by the light of very bright stars or planets. The NEO that almost hit Earth in 2002 approached from the direction of the sun. Against such a bright background, 2002 MN (only about 100 meters long) was impossible to see.

Lecture

I'm sure you've all seen movies recently in which asteroids threaten Earth. A movie called *Deep Impact* was one of them. In this movie, a high school student on a field trip spots a dangerous asteroid that threatens our planet. In real life, threatening asteroids are not discovered by teenagers. They are spotted by trained astronomers who know exactly what they are looking for.

These observers come from all sorts of places. The European Space Agency has some. So do most major observatories. By far, the largest group of them works for the National Aeronautics and Space Administration (NASA).

NASA has several teams of scientists scanning and recording the skies in search of NEOs. You can't just look at the sky once and say you've spotted an NEO. They look too much like stars. Instead, you have to record several images of the sky and see if anything is moving. In earlier times, ordinary photographs were used in this search. Astronomers took several pictures of the same area of the sky. Unknown objects that changed position from one picture to the next were probably NEOs. Those that changed position greatly were either moving very fast, were very close to Earth, or both. Brightness could indicate an NEO's size.

Modern teams of NEO trackers use machines called CCDs to take pictures of the sky. CCD images are digital and much more detailed than ordinary photographs. The analysis that used to be done by humans is now done by computers. Estimates of size, speed, and orbit track are calculated very carefully from the CCD images.

After an NEO's orbit is drawn by the computer, the object is given a name and categorized. Then the NEO is simply watched over and over again to check the computer's predictions and to see if it seems to threaten Earth.

Prompt Using information from both the reading and the lecture, describe NEOs and the process of discovering and tracking them.

Part 4 Expansion Activities

1 Creating Your Own Planet Create your own planet. It doesn't have to be in our solar system. First decide its name, where it is, how it was discovered, what its physical characteristics are, and whether it supports life forms. Then write an essay describing your planet.

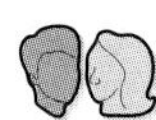

2 Guessing the Object Imagine that your classmate is from another planet and has never seen an object that you use every day. Write a paragraph describing the item, but do not include its name. Exchange paragraphs and guess the object that your partner described.

3 Discussing Inventions and Discoveries In small groups, talk about new discoveries and inventions you think will be made in the next 20 years. Have one person take notes during the discussion. Then follow these steps:

- Make a list of your discoveries and inventions.
- Discuss in which countries you think each of them will be made.
- Write the names of the countries next to each of the items.
- Put a check mark (✔) next to the discovery or invention that you believe will be the most important.
- Join another group of students and compare your lists.
- Discuss the similarities and differences as well as the reasons for your choices.

4 Writing in Your Journal Write for 15 minutes, answering one or both of the following questions:

1. Do you think governments should be spending a lot of money on space exploration? Why or why not?
2. Some people say that the oceans are the last unexplored frontier on Earth. Should we spend more time and money exploring our own planet rather than outer space? Why or why not?

5 Researching a Planet Search the Internet for more information about one aspect of the planet you wrote about. Find at least two facts that you didn't know before, and share them with your class.

Self-Assessment Log

In this chapter, you worked through the activities listed below. How much did they help you to become a better writer? Check *A lot, A little,* or *Not at all.*

	A lot	**A little**	**Not at all**
I learned to get information from charts and tables.	❑	❑	❑
I speculated about a planet.	❑	❑	❑
I used a graphic organizer to arrange ideas.	❑	❑	❑
I practiced organizing information in a descriptive essay.	❑	❑	❑
I learned to use the passive voice.	❑	❑	❑
I practiced varying sentence structure with introductory phrases.	❑	❑	❑
I learned to give reasons with *because* and *because of*.	❑	❑	❑
I used a writing rubric to evaluate my first draft.	❑	❑	❑
(Add something) ________________________________	❑	❑	❑

____

Ceremonies

In This Chapter

Genre Focus: Descriptive

Writing Product

A five-paragraph descriptive essay about a ceremony

Writing Process

- Write about facts and opinions.
- Use an outline to organize a five-paragraph essay.
- Learn to develop parallel body paragraphs.
- Practice writing effective introductions and conclusions.
- Practice identifying the passive voice and changing it to the active.
- Practice using pronouns.

"A graduation ceremony is an event where the commencement speaker tells thousands of students dressed in identical caps and gowns that 'individuality' is the key to success."

—Robert Orben
American humorist and writer (1927–)

Connecting to the Topic

1. What ceremony does the photo show?
2. Have you ever participated in or attended one of these ceremonies? Describe it.
3. What ceremony is most important to you?

Part 1 Before You Write

Exploring Ideas

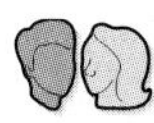

1 Discussing Ceremonies With a partner, think of as many different ceremonies as you can. Complete the chart below with information about the ceremonies.

Name of Ceremony	Approximate Age of Participants	Purpose of Ceremony

Building Vocabulary

2 Reading About Ceremonies Read the questions below. Then read the passage that follows, and answer the questions.

1. What are rites of passage?

____

____

2. Who was Arnold van Gennep?

____

____

3. What are the three steps in a rite of passage?

____

____

4. Which societies have rites of passage?

____

____

5. What are some common elements in a rite of passage?

____

____

Rites of passage are ceremonies that mark important periods of transition or change in a person's life. Some of these transitions are birth, puberty, marriage, having children, and death. The phrase *rite of passage* was first used by Belgian anthropologist Arnold van Gennep. He said that all rites of passage had three parts. First, the individual is separated from society. Then he or she undergoes a transformation. Finally, the participant returns to society with a different status.

▲ Many cultures consider giving birth a very important rite of passage.

Rites of passage occur in all societies. They often symbolically demonstrate the society's values. Some common symbolic elements are clothing, jewelry, words, music, and dance. In addition, the individual involved in the rite may have to prove himself or herself to the group he or she belongs to. In many societies, the most complex and significant rites of passage occur at puberty when young people move from childhood to adulthood.

3 Using a Vocabulary Chart

The chart below contains words from the reading passage above. Complete the table with the different forms of the words. Look in the dictionary for any words that you don't know.

Nouns	Verbs	Adjectives	Adverb
participant		XXXXXXXX	XXXXXXXX
		symbolic	symbolically
		individual	
transformation			XXXXXXXX
transition			XXXXXXXX
ceremony	XXXXXXXX		
	demonstrate	XXXXXXXX	XXXXXXXX
	prove		XXXXXXXX
		significant	

4 Using New Vocabulary

Use words from the table above to complete the sentences that follow.

1. A rite of passage marks an important <u>transition</u> from one stage of life to another.
2. Young people in many cultures ______________________ in a rite of passage to adulthood.

3. Participants in rites of passage often have to ______________________ themselves worthy of their new status.

4. During a rite of passage, a person ______________________ from one role to another. This ______________________ is mostly ______________________. The person's appearance is usually not changed.

5. In many Western societies, a wedding ring ______________________ marriage.

◀ The fast-breaking feast *Eid al-Fitr* is an important part of Ramadan.

Strategy

Distinguishing Between Facts and Opinions

In writing statements, you sometimes need to differentiate between fact and opinion.

For instance, the following statement is a fact:

Ramadan falls on a different date every year.

The following statement is an opinion:

The final fast-breaking feast called *Eid al-Fitr* is the most important part of Ramadan.

Because some people may disagree with the above opinion statement, it would be better to introduce the statement with a qualifier. A qualifier lets your reader know that you are stating an opinion or personal belief. It shows that you realize there may be differing opinions.

Some example qualifiers are:
In my opinion,
I think that
I believe that
To me,

These qualifiers don't have to be used every time you state an opinion, just in cases when you want to acknowledge that other opinions exist.

What Do You Think?

Distinguishing Between Facts and Opinions

Decide if each sentence below states an opinion or a fact. Rewrite the opinion statements using a qualifier.

1. Christmas is never celebrated in July.
   fact
2. A wedding is the most sacred rite of passage in one's life.
   ____
3. Graduation ceremonies are boring.
   ____
4. Rites of passage are not always happy events.
   ____
5. Baptisms should always take place in a church.
   ____
6. Graduation is the most important rite of passage for American teenagers.
   ____

Organizing Ideas

5 Free Writing Choose a ceremony to write about for your descriptive essay. Spend 10 minutes free writing about it. When you free write, don't worry about making mistakes; just write as much as you can. Try to capture as much detail about the ceremony as possible.

Using Graphic Organizers

6 Using Graphic Organizers Complete the following chart with information about the ceremony you chose to write about.

Clothing	Words	Music	Action	Other

Strategy

Using an Outline to Develop a Five-Paragraph Essay

A five-paragraph essay includes an introduction, three body paragraphs, and a conclusion. The three body paragraphs should be parallel. That means, the subtopics for each paragraph should be presented in the same order. For instance, if you are writing about the music, clothing, and diploma used in a graduation ceremony, you'll write one paragraph for each of these topics. Within these paragraphs, you'll address two or three subtopics. The subtopics will appear in the same order in each paragraph. Creating an outline is one of the best ways to plan how you will present the information in your body paragraphs.

Look at the outline below. Although paragraphs B, C, and D are about different topics, the information in each follows a similar pattern; it is delivered in the same order. This means that paragraphs B, C, and D are parallel.

A. Introduction

B. Music
- description
- significance

C. Clothing
- description
- significance

D. Diploma
- description
- significance

E. Conclusion

7 **Evaluating an Outline** Answer the following questions about the outline above:

1. What topics will each paragraph discuss?

   ____

2. What information will be given about each topic?

   ____

8 **Analyzing Body Paragraphs** Read the essay that follows. Fill in sections B, C, and D of the outline above with information from the essay. Discuss your answers with a partner.

▲ Graduation is an important rite of passage in the United States.

One of the most important rites of passage in American society is graduation. Graduation ceremonies mark the end of a course of study. Many American students go through several graduation ceremonies in their lifetimes including elementary school, middle school, high school, college, and graduate school. All graduation ceremonies have three things in common: music, clothing, and a diploma.

The standard music at graduation ceremonies is a processional. The processional is usually played while the participants slowly walk into, and then out of, the ceremony. In the United States, a piece called "Pomp and Circumstance," by British composer Sir Edward Elgar, is usually played. This solemn and dramatic composition symbolizes the importance of the graduation ceremony.

Another very important element of graduation ceremonies is special dress. The graduates wear caps and gowns that completely cover their clothing. In the past, the gowns were always black, but today they are usually the school colors. On their heads, graduates wear a cap with a square, flat top. It usually has a colored tassel that hangs down in the front. The gown was the traditional clothing of students and professors hundreds of years ago, so it signifies that the wearer is an academic. And the cap signifies the student's change in status when, at the end of the graduation ceremony, the participants move the tassel from left to right.

Finally, perhaps the most important element of the graduation ceremony is the diploma. During the graduation ceremony, each student's name is called. Then he or she comes to the front of the group and is given the diploma. This is the piece of paper that proves that the individual has graduated.

To me, graduation symbolizes the importance of education in American society. I believe that it is also an important rite of passage for all students because it marks the beginning of their lives as productive adult members of society. That is why a graduation ceremony is often called a *commencement.* It is the beginning of a new stage in life.

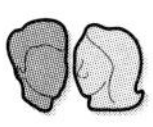

9 **Analyzing an Introduction and Conclusion** With a partner, look at the introduction and conclusion in the essay above. Discuss what type of information is included in the introduction and conclusion, and fill in sections A and D of the outline on page 184 with notes from your discussion.

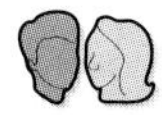

10 Creating an Outline Create an outline for your five-paragraph descriptive essay. Use the outline on page 184 as a model. Share your outline with a partner and discuss your organization.

TOEFL® IBT

Focus on Testing

Making Connections Between Readings and Lectures

As you saw in Chapter 9, you will be given a reading and a lecture for the integrated writing task on the TOEFL® Internet-Based Test (iBT). Your response must refer to both of these sources.

The prompts for the integrated writing task will ask you to make some kind of connection between the reading and the lecture. It will ask one of the following:

- How does the lecture support the reading?
- In what ways does the lecture cast doubt on information from the reading?*
- What did you learn about the topic from both the reading and the lecture?

*The verb phrase *cast doubt on* means *to make something seem untrue*.

The following note-taking strategies can help you see relationships between the reading and the listening passage:

1. Make two sections in your notes—one for the reading, the other for the lecture. These two sections should appear side-by-side. The best method is to use one clean sheet of notepaper with a line drawn down the middle of the sheet from top to bottom. Label the left side *reading* and the right side *lecture*. If your handwriting is large, use two whole sheets of paper instead of two halves of a single sheet.
2. Never take notes on the back of notepaper. Flipping pages over is a waste of time and breaks your concentration.
3. Your reading notes can provide a structure for your listening notes. When a point in the lecture relates to a point in the reading, write your lecture note next to the related reading point.
4. If you realize that a lecture point relates to a reading point, draw a line connecting the two.

Practice Give yourself 5 minutes to take notes on the reading that follows. Then allow 3 minutes to take notes on the lecture. Compare your notes to those taken by another student. Discuss the differences between the two sets of notes.

Reading

In many places around the world, plants cannot grow all year long. In these places, as summer turns to autumn, the growing season ends, and farmers harvest (gather up) the crops they have grown. At this time, with fresh food easily available, a ceremony called a *harvest festival* may be held.

Nearly every society where crops are seasonal celebrates the harvest. In the United States and Canada, Thanksgiving is a harvest festival, as is the Choksu Festival in Korea, the August Moon Festival in China, the Yam Festival in West Africa, and the Pongal Festival in India. At each of these festivals, the focus is on food such as turkeys and cranberry sauce, rice dishes, yams, or round moon-shaped cakes. During a harvest festival, even people who aren't involved in agriculture express their gratitude for what farmers have been able to produce.

Most harvest festivals involve either family gatherings or large community celebrations. The sense of community is important. Much of it probably comes from the approach of winter—a time when survival is not certain. Everyone needs a family and a community as the weather turns cold and the food supplies get smaller.

Lecture

Very few modern societies are mostly agricultural. And, even in countries with large agricultural businesses, like Argentina or the United States, most people live in cities. It is a mistake to say that such societies have harvest festivals at the end of the growing season. Few people who celebrate Thanksgiving in the United States, for example, are even aware that harvest time has come to a close. After all, they buy the same products in grocery stores year-round.

It is more accurate to call such celebrations *autumn festivals*. What do these festivals mean to most people who celebrate them? In the United States, Thanksgiving means food, parades, football on television, and family gatherings. Chusok in Korea means family gatherings, reverence for ancestors, and fancy clothing. The August Moon Festival in China means moon-shaped cakes, offerings to hungry ghosts, and the family getting together. None of this has anything to do with the harvest.

True harvest festivals can be found only in very rural places such as Kyrgyzstan or southern Poland. There, the people celebrating are the ones who actually planted and harvested the crops. When they celebrate a harvest, it is out of real gratitude

Part 2 Developing Writing Skills

Developing Cohesion and Clarity

AVOIDING THE PASSIVE VOICE

In Chapter 9, you learned that the passive voice is frequently used in scientific writing. There are also some phrases such as *be named* and *be born* that are almost always used in the passive voice.

Examples

My father was named after President Kennedy. I was born in Hollywood, California.

Because the passive voice makes your writing less active, and therefore less interesting, it is better to write in the active voice whenever possible. In the active voice, the subject of the sentence does the action and the object receives the action.

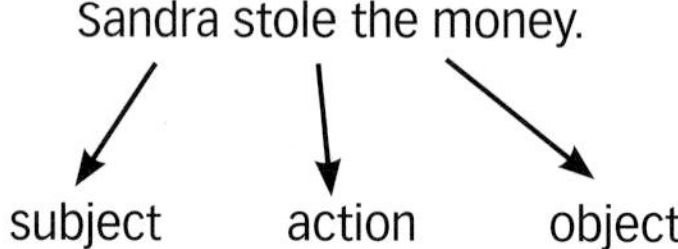

With the active voice, readers can clearly see who is responsible for the action in a sentence.

1 Rewriting Sentences in the Active Voice Rewrite the sentences below so that they are in the active voice.

1. A new car was bought, and a trip to Europe was taken by Diane.
   Diane bought a new car and took a trip to Europe.
   ____
2. The class was divided into two groups of 15 by the teacher.
   ____
   ____
3. At the end of the ceremony, the married couple is cheered by their friends and family.
   ____
   ____
4. The break-in was detected by our new high-tech alarm system.
   ____
   ____

5. The examination was failed by almost 50% of the class.

____

____

6. Many homes were destroyed by hurricane Katrina.

____

____

7. At some weddings, a white dress and veil are worn by the bride.

____

____

8. In a baptism, water is poured on the baby's head by a priest, a minister, or other religious official.

____

____

PRONOUNS

You are familiar with personal pronouns such as *he, she,* and *it.* However, a number of other words can be used as pronouns as well.

Look at the sentences below. What do the underlined words refer to?

1. There were four speeches at my graduation. Three were good, but the fourth was terrible.
2. I missed both my elementary and high school graduation ceremonies. I was sick for one and out of town for the other.
3. My family gathers for only two occasions: weddings and funerals. Of course, everyone prefers the former to the latter.

Note: *The former* means the first thing mentioned and *the latter* means the second thing.

4. Music is an important part of a graduation ceremony. Clothing is another.
5. Some graduation speakers are entertaining but might not say anything memorable. Others actually try to give the graduates some ideas to remember.

2 Rewriting Sentences Using Pronouns Rewrite the sentences below by replacing some of the subjects with pronouns. Share your answers with a partner. More than one answer is possible.

1. Students display different emotions at graduation ceremonies. Some students are relieved, and some students are bored.

Students and their families display different emotions at graduation.

Some students are relieved, and some are bored.

____

2. A baptism and a funeral are like bookends. A baptism celebrates the beginning of a life, and a funeral marks the end of a life.

____

____

____

3. Three students gave speeches at my graduation. Mary was the first speaker. George was the second speaker. Larry was the last speaker. Mary and George's speeches were terrible. Mary's speech was boring. George's speech was impossible to understand. Larry's speech was great.

____

____

____

4. There are two rites of passage that we have no say about. One rite of passage is baptism, which, for many people, takes place when they are infants. The other rite of passage is a funeral, which takes place after death.

____

____

____

3 Writing the First Draft Write your five-paragraph descriptive essay about a ceremony. Use the outline and notes you developed earlier in the chapter.

Part 3 Revising and Editing

Revising for Content and Editing for Form

1 Revising for Content Read the questions below. Then revise the paragraph that follows for content. Use your answers to the questions to guide you.

1. What is the introduction missing?
2. What is the focus of each of the body paragraphs?
3. What pattern is used to present information in each paragraph?
4. What is the conclusion missing?

The most familiar rite of passage in the United States is the wedding ceremony. Almost everyone participates in at least one wedding ceremony in his or her lifetime. The Western wedding ceremony is also familiar to those who do not live in the United States because it is commonplace in movies and television programs.

▲ Western wedding ceremonies are familiar to many people around the world.

One element of a traditional Western wedding is the clothing. White dresses with veils are worn by many brides. White symbolizes purity. The veil, which is lifted from the bride's face during the ceremony, comes from the time when the bride and groom were introduced during the wedding ceremony. The bride also carries flowers.

Another element is the involvement of friends and family. Several friends and family participate in the planning of the ceremony and the ceremony itself. The bride chooses at least one friend to be a bridesmaid. The groom chooses a best man. These two people help the bride and groom on this important day. For example, traditionally the ring is held by the best man during the ceremony. In addition to these two people, there may be several others who act as bridesmaids and groomsmen. Large weddings may also include a flower girl and a ring-bearer. The father of the bride also has an important part in the ceremony. The bride is escorted into the ceremony and then "given away" to the groom by her father.

The most important part of the ceremony is the reciting of the wedding vows. Vows are promises that the bride and groom make to each other in front of their friends and family. Traditional religious vows are chosen by some couples. Others couples choose to write their vows themselves. After they say their vows, the couple is considered married. It is not unusual for those attending the wedding to cheer the new couple at this point.

Weddings are generally joyous occasions. They are ceremonies of hope and new beginnings that symbolize the creation of a new family unit and the possibility of future generations.

2 Editing for Form Now identify and fix the sentences in the essay in which the passive voice should be changed to the active voice.

Evaluating Your Writing

3 **Using a Rubric** Read the rubric below with your class. Then use the rubric to score your essay.

Score	Description
3 **Excellent**	▪ **Content:** Essay describes a ceremony and gives interesting details about three aspects of the ceremony. ▪ **Organization:** Essay includes five paragraphs including an introduction, conclusion, and three body paragraphs that present information in a similar pattern. ▪ **Vocabulary:** Vocabulary is specific, descriptive, and used correctly throughout. ▪ **Grammar:** Pronouns are used correctly, and passive voice is avoided. ▪ **Spelling and Mechanics:** Words are spelled correctly, and punctuation is correct.
2 **Adequate**	▪ **Content:** Essay describes a ceremony and gives some details about aspects of the ceremony. Some details may be unclear or limited. ▪ **Organization:** Essay includes five paragraphs, but organization is unclear. Some information may be missing from the introduction or the conclusion. ▪ **Vocabulary:** Vocabulary is specific and descriptive, but some words are used incorrectly. ▪ **Grammar:** Some pronouns are used incorrectly, and passive voice may be used too often. ▪ **Spelling and Mechanics:** Essay includes some spelling and punctuation mistakes.
1 **Developing**	▪ **Content:** Essay does not include five paragraphs. Details about the ceremony are lacking. ▪ **Organization:** One or more body paragraphs are missing. Order of information is unclear. Several elements of introduction and concluding paragraphs are missing. ▪ **Vocabulary:** Vocabulary is limited, or there are too many mistakes to understand the ideas. ▪ **Grammar:** Pronouns are not used. Many grammar errors make the essay difficult to understand. ▪ **Spelling and Mechanics:** Essay includes many distracting spelling and punctuation mistakes.

WRITING WITH COMPUTERS

When you are writing or revising your essay, you can switch views in order to see your essay in different formats. With most word processing programs, you can go to **File** and click **Print Layout** to see your essay laid out across one or more pages. From there you can also adjust margins and add page numbers.

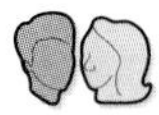

4 **Peer Sharing** Exchange essays with a classmate. Read about the ceremony your partner described. Does it conform to Van Gennep's description of a rite of passage? Why or why not?

5 **Writing the Second Draft** Rewrite your essay using your rubric evaluation. Revise for content, and edit for form. Then give your essay to your teacher for comments. When your teacher returns your paper, ask him or her about any comments you don't understand.

Part 4 Expansion Activities

1 **Interview Someone About His or Her Wedding** Interview your parents, grandparents, or friends about their wedding ceremony. How was it the same or different from wedding ceremonies today? Have the traditions changed?

2 **Making a Display** Create a display of a rite of passage including photographs or drawings. Share it with the class.

3 **Writing in Your Journal** Write in your journal for 10 or 15 minutes, answering one or both of the following questions:

1. Are rites of passage important to you? Why or why not?
2. Describe a rite of passage that is different from the one you wrote about.

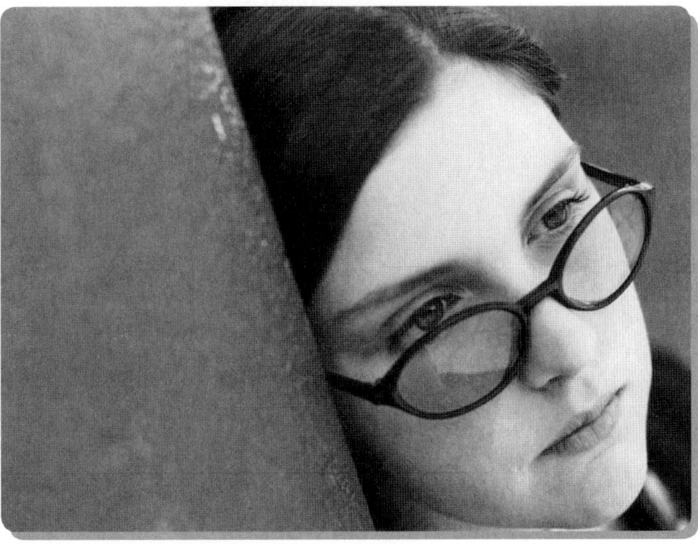

▲ Adolescence is an important rite of passage.

4 **Researching a Rite of Passage** Find information about a rite of passage from a different culture or religion. Search with these terms: *rite of passage* + *ceremony* + (country or religion). Read about the rite of passage, and complete the table below. Share the information with your classmates.

Name of Ceremony	Participants	Purpose	Description			
			Clothing	Music	Actions	Words

▲ A Japanese woman prepares tea for a tea ceremony.

Self-Assessment Log

In this chapter, you worked through the activities listed below. How much did they help you to become a better writer? Check *A lot, A little,* or *Not at all.*

	A lot	**A little**	**Not at all**
I wrote about facts and opinions.	❑	❑	❑
I used an outline to organize my five-paragraph essay.	❑	❑	❑
I learned to develop parallel body paragraphs.	❑	❑	❑
I practiced writing effective introductions and conclusions.	❑	❑	❑
I learned to avoid the passive voice.	❑	❑	❑
I practiced using pronouns to make my writing flow better.	❑	❑	❑
I used a writing rubric to evaluate my first draft.	❑	❑	❑
(Add something) ______________________________	❑	❑	❑

____

Appendix 1

Spelling Rules for Adding Endings

Endings That Begin with Vowels (*-ed, -ing, -er, -est*)

1. For words ending in silent *e*, drop the *e* and add the ending.

   lik**e** → lik**ed** mak**e** → mak**ing** saf**e** → saf**er** fin**e** → fin**est**

2. For one-syllable words ending in a single vowel and a single consonant, double the final consonant, and add the ending.

   b**at** → bat**ted** r**un** → run**ning** f**at** → fat**ter** h**ot** → hot**test**

3. Don't double the final consonant when the word has two final consonants or two vowels before a final consonant.

   pi**ck** → pic**ked** si**ng** → sin**ging** cl**ea**n → clea**ner** c**oo**l → coo**lest**

4. For words of two or more syllables that end in a single vowel and a single consonant, double the final consonant if the stress is on the final syllable.

   ref**er** → refe**rred** beg**in** → begin**ning** beg**in** → begin**ner**

5. For words of two or more syllables that end in a single vowel and a single consonant, make no change if the stress is not on the final syllable.

   trav**el** → trave**led** trav**el** → trave**ling**
   trav**el** → trave**ler** yell**ow** → yello**west**

6. For words ending in a consonant and *y*, change the *y* to *i* and add the ending unless the ending begins with *i*.

   stu**dy** → stud**ied** dirt**y** → dirt**ier** sunn**y** → sunn**iest**
   stu**dy** → stud**ying** hurr**y** → hurr**ying**

7. For words ending in a vowel and *y*, make no change before adding the ending.

   pl**ay** → play**ed** st**ay** → stay**ing** pl**ay** → play**er** gr**ay** → gray**est**

Endings That Begin with Consonants (*-ly, -ment*)

1. For words ending in a silent *e*, make no change when adding endings that begin with consonants.

   fin**e** → fin**ely** stat**e** → stat**ement**

2. For words ending in a consonant and *y*, change the *y* to *i* before adding the ending.

   hap**py** → happ**ily** mer**ry** → merr**iment**

Adding a Final *s* to Nouns and Verbs

1. Generally, add the *s* without making changes.

   sit → sit**s** dance → dance**s** play → play**s** book → book**s**

2. If a word ends in a consonant and *y*, change the *y* to *i* and add *es*.

   mar**ry** → marr**ies** stu**dy** → stud**ies** cher**ry** → cherr**ies**

3. If word ends in *ch*, *s*, *sh*, *x*, or *z*, add *es*.

   chur**ch** → church**es** ca**sh** → cash**es** fiz**z** → fizz**es**
   bos**s** → boss**es** mi**x** → mix**es**

4. For words ending in *o*, sometimes add *es* and sometimes add *s*.

   tomat**o** → tomato**es** potat**o** → potato**es**
   pian**o** → piano**s** radi**o** → radio**s**

5. For words ending in *f* or *fe*, generally drop the *f* or *fe* and add *ves*.

   hal**f** → hal**ves** kni**fe** → kni**ves**

   Exceptions: sa**fe** → safe**s** roo**f** → roof**s**

Appendix 2

Capitalization Rules

First Words

1. Capitalize the first word of every sentence.

   They live near my house. **W**hat is it?

2. Capitalize the first word of a quotation that is a full sentence.

   He said, "**M**y name is Paul." Jenny asked, "**W**hen is the party?"

Personal Names

1. Capitalize the names of people including initials and titles.

   Mrs. **J**ones **M**ohandas **G**andhi **J**ohn **F**. **K**ennedy

2. Capitalize family words if they appear alone or followed by a name.

   Let's go, **D**ad. Where's **G**randma? She's at **A**unt **L**ucy's.

3. Don't capitalize family words with a possessive pronoun or article.

   my **u**ncle her **m**other our **g**randparents an **a**unt

4. Capitalize the pronoun *I*.

   I have a book. She's bigger than **I** am.

5. Capitalize the names of nationalities, races, peoples, and religions.

   Japanese **A**rab **A**sian **C**hicano **M**uslim

6. Generally, don't capitalize occupations.

   I am a **s**ecretary. She wants to be a **l**awyer.

Place Names

1. Capitalize the names of countries, states, provinces, and cities.

   Lebanon **N**ew **Y**ork **Q**uebec **I**stanbul

2. Capitalize the names of oceans, lakes, rivers, islands, and mountains.

   the **A**tlantic **O**cean **L**ake **C**omo the **N**ile **R**iver
   Maui **M**t. **A**rarat

3. Capitalize the names of geographical areas.

   the **S**outh the **M**iddle **E**ast **A**frica **A**ntarctica

4. Don't capitalize directions if they aren't names of geographical areas.

   He lives **e**ast of Toronto. We walked **s**outhwest.

5. Capitalize names of schools, parks, buildings, and streets.

   the **U**niversity of **G**eorgia **C**entral **P**ark
   the **S**ears **B**uilding **O**xford **R**oad

Time Words

1. Capitalize names of days and months.

   Monday **F**riday **J**anuary **M**arch

2. Capitalize names of holidays and historical events.

   Independence **D**ay **W**orld **W**ar II

3. Don't capitalize names of seasons.

   spring **s**ummer **f**all **w**inter

Titles

1. Capitalize the first word and all important words of titles of books, magazines, newspapers, songs, and articles.

   ***I**nteractions* ***T**he **N**ew **Y**ork **T**imes* "**T**raveling in **E**gypt"

2. Capitalize the first word and all important words in titles of movies, plays, radio programs, and television programs.

   ***T**he **M**atrix* ***T**he **T**empest* ***N**ews **R**oundup* ***T**he **S**impsons*

3. Don't capitalize articles (*a*, *an*, *the*) conjunctions (*but*, *and*, *or*) or short prepositions (*of*, *with*, *in*, *on*, *for*) unless they are the first word of a title.
   ***T**he Life **o**f Pi* *War **a**nd Peace* *Death **o**f **a** Salesman*

Names of Organizations

1. Capitalize the names of organizations, government groups, and businesses.

   International **S**tudent **A**ssociation   the **S**enate   **G**oogle™

2. Capitalize brand names, but do not capitalize the names of the product.

   IBM™ computer   **T**oyota™ truck   **K**ellogg's™ cereal

Other

1. Capitalize the names of languages.

   Arabic   **S**panish   **T**hai   **J**apanese

2. Don't capitalize school subjects unless they are the names of languages or are followed by a number.

   geometry   **m**usic   **E**nglish   **W**riting 101   **H**istory 211

Appendix 3

Punctuation Rules

Period

1. Use a period after a statement or command.

   We are studying English.   Open your books to Chapter 3.

2. Use a period after most abbreviations.

   Mr.   Ms.   Dr.   Ave.   etc.

3. Use a period after initials.

   H. G. Wells   Dr. H. R. Hammond

Question Mark

1. Use a question mark after (not before) questions.

   Where are you going?   Is he here yet?

2. In a direct quotation, the question mark goes before the quotation marks.

   He asked, "What's your name?"

Exclamation Point

Use an exclamation point after exclamatory sentences or phrases.

Let the students vote!   Be quiet!   Wow!

*In academic writing, exclamation points are very rare.

Comma

1. Use a comma before a conjunction (*and*, *or*, *so*, *but*) that separates two independent clauses.

   She wanted to work, so she decided to study English.
   He wasn't happy in his apartment, but he didn't have the money to move.

2. Don't use a comma before a conjunction that separates two phrases that aren't complete sentences.

   She worked in the library and studied at night.
   Do you want to go to a movie or stay home?

3. Use a comma after an introductory phrase (generally, if it is five or more words long).

   During the long summer vacation, I decided to learn Chinese.
   After a beautiful wedding ceremony, they had a reception in her mother's home.

   If you want to write well, you should practice often.

4. Use a comma to separate interrupting expressions from the rest of a sentence.

   Do you know, by the way, what time dinner is?
   Many of the students, I found out, stayed on campus during the holidays.

5. Use a comma after transition words and phrases.

   In addition, he stole all her jewelry.
   Common transitional words and phrases are:

also	for this reason	in addition	on the other hand
besides	for instance	in fact	similarly
consequently	furthermore	moreover	therefore
for example	however	nevertheless	

6. Use a comma to separate names of people in direct address from the rest of a sentence.

   Jane, have you seen Paul?
   We aren't sure where he is, Ms. Green.

7. Use a comma after *yes* and *no* in answers.

   Yes, he was here a minute ago.
   No, I haven't.

8. Use a comma to separate items in a series.

   We have coffee, tea, and milk.
   He looked in the refrigerator, on the shelves, and in the cupboard.

9. Use a comma to separate an appositive from the rest of a sentence.

   Mrs. Sampson, his English teacher, gave him a bad grade.
   Would you like to try a taco, a delicious Mexican food?

10. If a date or address has two or more parts, use a comma after each part.

    I was born on June 5, 1968.
    The house at 230 Seventh Street, Miami, Florida is for sale.

11. Use a comma to separate contrasting information from the rest of the sentence.

    It wasn't Jamila, but Fatima, who was absent.
    Bring your writing book, not your reading book.

12. Use a comma to separate quotations from the rest of a sentence.

    He asked, "What are we going to do?"
    "I didn't have enough money," she explained.

13. Use a comma to separate two or more adjectives that each modify the noun alone.

    She was an intelligent, beautiful actress. (*intelligent* and *beautiful* actress)
    Eat those delicious green beans. (*delicious* modifies *green beans*)

14. Use a comma to separate nonrestrictive clauses from the rest of a sentence. A nonrestrictive clause gives more information about the noun it describes, but it isn't needed to identify the noun. Clauses after proper names are nonrestrictive and require commas.

    It's a Wonderful Life, which is often on television at Christmas time, is my favorite movie.
    James Stewart, who plays a depressed man thinking of ending his life, received an Academy Award for his performance.

Semicolons

1. A semicolon is often an alternative to a period. Use a semicolon between two sentences that are very closely related.

   I'm sure Dan is at home; he never goes out on school nights.

2. Use a semicolon before transition words and phrases such as *however*, *therefore*, *nevertheless*, *furthermore*, *for example*, *as a result*, *that is*, and *in fact*.

   Malaria is a major health problem around the world; however, some progress is being made in developing low-cost treatments for it.

Quotation Marks

1. Use quotation marks at the beginning and end of exact quotations. Other punctuation marks go before the end quotation marks.

   He said, "I'm going to Montreal."
   "How are you traveling to France?" he asked.

2. Use quotation marks before and after titles of works that appear within larger works: short stories, articles, and songs. Periods and commas go before the final quotation marks.

   My favorite song is "Let it Be."

Apostrophes

1. Use apostrophes in contractions.

   don't it's* we've they're

*Notice the difference between: It's hot. (*It's* is a contraction of *it is*.) The dog is hurt. Its leg is broken. (*Its* is possessive.)

2. Use an apostrophe to make possessive nouns.

   Singular: Jerry's my boss's
   Plural: the children's the Smiths'

Underlining and Italicizing

The tiles of books, magazines, newspapers, plays, television programs, and movies should be italicized. If italicizing is not possible because you are writing by hand, underline instead.

I am reading *One Hundred Years of Solitude*.
Did you like the movie *Crash*?

Appendix 4

A List of Noncount Nouns

Food

bread, butter, cheese, chicken*, chocolate, coffee,* cream, fish,* flour, fruit, ice cream,* juice, meat, milk, rice, salt, spaghetti, sugar, tea

Activities and Sports

baseball,* chess, dance,* skating, soccer, tennis

* These nouns have both count and noncount uses. They are noncount when they refer to the item in general. They are count when they refer to a particular item.

I love chicken. (the meat)
The farmer raised twenty chickens. (the animals)
Coffee is delicious. (the drink)
Can I have a coffee please? (a cup of coffee)

Natural Phenomena

Weather:	rain, snow, sunshine, thunder, wind
Gases:	air, hydrogen, nitrogen, oxygen
Minerals:	copper, gold, iron, silver, steel
Materials:	dirt, dust, grass, ice, land, oil, sand, water

Emotions and Qualities**

ambition, anger, courage, fear, freedom, happiness, hatred, honesty, justice, loneliness, love, joy, pride

Social Issues**

abortion, crime, democracy, divorce, freedom, hunger, nuclear power, peace, pollution, poverty

Mass Nouns (Composed of Dissimilar items)

change, clothing, fruit, equipment, furniture, information, jewelry, luggage, mail, machinery, makeup, medicine, money, noise, scenery, technology, transportation, vocabulary

Subjects

art, economics, history, humanities, physics

Miscellaneous

advice, business, fun, glass, homework, knowledge, information, insurance, life, nature, news, paint, publicity, reality, research, sleep, time, traffic, trouble, tuition, work

** Most emotions, qualities, and social issue nouns can also function as count nouns: a strong ambition, a deep hatred, a terrible crime, a young democracy

Appendix 5

Subordinating Conjunctions

Subordinating conjunctions can show relationships of time, reason, contrast, and purpose.

1. Time: when, whenever
2. Reason: because, since
3. Contrast: although, even though, though
4. Purpose: so that

Appendix 6

Transitions

Transitions are words or phrases that show the relationship between two ideas. The most common transitions are used to:

1. Give examples: for example, for instance
2. Add emphasis: in fact, of course
3. Add information: in addition, furthermore, moreover, besides
4. Make comparisons: similarly, likewise
5. Show contrast: however, nevertheless, in contrast, on the contrary, on one/on the other hand
6. Give reasons or results: therefore, as a result, as a consequence, for this/that reason
7. Show sequences: now, then, first (second, etc.) earlier, later, meanwhile, finally